Income Redistribution, Inequality and Democracy

This book examines why democracy has failed to deliver effective solutions to income inequality problems over the last four decades, and if democracy can offer solutions to various increases in inequality in the future. It also addresses what elements are necessary for democracy to serve as an effective alternative for addressing inequality issues.

Historical experiences over the past 40 years, including the global financial crisis, not only underscore the need for fresh perspectives on income inequality in economics but also question the ability of democracy to continue providing alternatives for addressing the escalating forms of inequality. Seo and Kang's response to these inquiries diverge from conventional research in several significant ways. Primarily, what sets this research apart from existing studies is its intensified focus on income inequality as a product of the complex interplay between the political and economic domains, rather than a standalone examination of income inequality in isolation. Through a political economy perspective, this book argues that income inequality and income redistribution are shaped by the institutions, policies, and laws generated by the political system, with their formation and nature being determined by the power distribution among socio-political groups.

A useful resource not only to researchers who study political phenomena in the field of economics, but also to scholars who study economic phenomena in the field of politics. Furthermore, it will be particularly intriguing for policy makers concerned with issues of inequality and income redistribution.

Hwan Joo Seo is Professor at the Division of Business Administration at Hanyang University ERICA Campus, South Korea. He received his PhD in Economics at École des hautes études en sciences sociales in 1998. His research interests focus on the theory of régulation, income equality, and political economy.

Sung Jin Kang is Professor in the Department of Economics at Korea University. He received PhD in Economics at Stanford University in 1999. Recently his research has focused on green finance, low carbon transition and global green trade, sustainable development, etc.

Routledge Frontiers of Political Economy

Political Economy of the Spanish Miracle
State, Labor and Capital, 1931–1973
Diego Ayala

Heterodox Economics and Global Emergencies
Voices from Around the World
Edited by Ariane Agunsoye, Thoralf Dassler, Eurydice Fotopoulou and Jon Mulberg

Political Economy of the Firm
Authority, Governance, and Economic Democracy
Helena Lopes and Christophe Clerc

Digital Capitalism and New Institutionalism
Daniil Frolov

What Is Financialization?
Taner Akan and Halil İbrahim Gündüz

Unequal Development and Capitalism
Catching up and Falling behind in the Global Economy
Alessandro Donadio Miebach, Henrique Morrone and Adalmir Marquetti

Economic Growth and Long Cycles
A Classical Political Economy Approach
Nikolaos Chatzarakis, Persefoni Tsaliki and Lefteris Tsoulfidis

Income Redistribution, Inequality and Democracy
A Political Economy Approach
Hwan Joo Seo and Sung Jin Kang

For more information about this series, please visit: www.routledge.com/Routledge-Frontiers-of-Political-Economy/book-series/SE0345

Income Redistribution, Inequality and Democracy

A Political Economy Approach

Hwan Joo Seo and Sung Jin Kang

Routledge
Taylor & Francis Group
LONDON AND NEW YORK

First published 2024
by Routledge
4 Park Square, Milton Park, Abingdon, Oxon, OX14 4RN

and by Routledge
605 Third Avenue, New York, NY 10158

Routledge is an imprint of the Taylor & Francis Group, an informa business

British Library Cataloguing-in-Publication Data
A catalogue record for this book is available from the British Library

Library of Congress Cataloging-in-Publication Data
Names: Hwan, Joo Seo, author. | Sung, Jin Kang, author.
Title: Income redistribution, inequality and democracy : a political economy approach / Joo Seo Hwan and Jin Kang Sung.
Description: First edition. | New York, NY : Routledge, 2024.|
Series: Routledge frontiers of political economy | Includes bibliographical references and index
Identifiers: LCCN 2023056994 (print) | LCCN 2023056995 (ebook) | ISBN 9781032695778 (hardback) | ISBN 9781032695761 (paperback) | ISBN 9781032695754 (ebook)
Subjects: LCSH: Income distribution. | Democracy--Economic aspects.
Classification: LCC HC79.I5 H93 2024 (print) | LCC HC79.I5 (ebook) | DDC 339.2--dc23/eng/20231208
LC record available at https://lccn.loc.gov/2023056994
LC ebook record available at https://lccn.loc.gov/2023056995

ISBN: 978-1-032-69577-8 (hbk)
ISBN: 978-1-032-69576-1 (pbk)
ISBN: 978-1-032-69575-4 (ebk)

DOI: 10.4324/9781032695754

Typeset in Galliard
by SPi Technologies India Pvt Ltd (Straive)

Contents

Figures

Tables

1 Introduction

1.1 What insights have researchers gained from the global financial crisis?

Mainstream economics has traditionally held a somewhat optimistic view of income inequality, based on two primary justifications. The first justification, following Okun (1975), posits that income inequality positively contributes to growth and innovation. Okun, frequently cited as a basis for critiquing the welfare state or validating neoliberal policies, argued in his book *Equality and Efficiency: The Big Trade-off* that inequality motivates economic agents. This motivation, in turn, stimulates the desire to work, and encourages capital accumulation and technological innovation, thereby making a positive contribution to economic growth. The second justification, based on the hypothesis of M-R (Meltzer & Richard 1981), contends that even if income inequality increases, democratic nations can address the issue through income redistribution policies. In democratic nations where each citizen is granted equal voting rights, income inequality can be mitigated through voting, as combination of low-income and middle-income groups constitutes the majority. Thus, even if income inequality escalates, voters can support parties advocating income redistribution policies through their ballots, leading to a potential solution to the income inequality problem. Therefore, according to mainstream economics, a certain level of income inequality not only positively impacts the economy but also carries the optimistic expectation that, in democratic countries, income inequality can be adjusted through income redistribution policies due to the self-correcting mechanism of elections.

However, the global financial crisis that occurred between 2007 and 2008 has cast doubt on these optimistic perspectives on income inequality and revealed new insights about it. First, observers have noted that the previous wave of growth did not "float all boats." Contrary to the assumptions of the trickle-down effect theory championed by neoliberals, economic growth does not inherently resolve the issue of income inequality. Moreover, diverging from Okun's expectations, escalating income inequality jeopardizes the stability of the economy and can ultimately precipitate economic crises (Ostry et al., 2014; Tridico, 2012; Stockhammer, 2012). Secondly, in contrast to M-R hypothesis

DOI: 10.4324/9781032695754-1

expectations, democratic countries have not enacted significant income redistribution policies over the past four decades, despite escalating income inequality. As a result, income inequality persists and, in fact, precipitates crises within democratic systems. Thirdly, not only income inequality, but also political and opportunity inequality have been concurrently escalating. With the rise in income inequality, the economic and political clout of the affluent elite expands, culminating in a scenario where not all citizens wield equal influence over government policies. Furthermore, government policies tend to be more attuned to the voices of the wealthy, rather than those of the low-income or middle-income groups (The American Political Science Association Task Force, 2004). In other words, current research recognizes that political inequality is on the rise. Moreover, recent studies (Stiglitz, 2012; Corak, 2013) highlight that opportunity inequality is also markedly on the rise, and that this inequality is perpetuated across generations. As Rawls (1999) emphasizes in *A Theory of Justice*, equal opportunity forms the basis of social justice, and for this to hold true, individual achievement and income must not be affected by factors such as race, gender, and family background. In other words, individuals of like talent should be able to dream of similar futures. However, Corak (2013) finds that income inequality and inequality of opportunity are closely related, and that family background and parental socioeconomic status exert a greater impact on children's income today than in the past.

> As a result of the global financial crisis, researchers have come to recognize that income inequality, political inequality, and inequality of opportunity are all rising concurrently, and that these increases are cumulative as one inequality serves as a catalyst for the emergence of additional inequalities. Moreover, economists have recognized, contrary to their expectations, that even with the concurrent rise in various forms of inequality, neither the trickle-down effect nor the equalizing effect of democracy came into play. Instead, they understand that the escalation of inequality led to more than just economic crises; it precipitated a crisis for democracy itself.

These historical experiences not only underscore the need for fresh perspectives on income inequality in economics but also question the ability of democracy to continue providing alternatives for addressing the escalating forms of inequality. Therefore, this book aims to pose the following questions and seek answers to them, beginning with an awareness of the gravity of these issues:

1 Why, contrary to expectations, has democracy failed to deliver effective solutions to income inequality problems over the last four decades?
2 Can democracy offer a solution to various increases in inequality, including income inequality, in the future? And what elements are necessary for democracy to serve as an effective alternative for addressing inequality issues?

To unearth answers to these inquiries, the book embarks on exploring the following themes:

1. Firstly, it strives to identify the diverse manifestations of expanding inequalities.
2. Secondly, it undertakes a systematic examination of the M-R model, which provides evidence that democracy can serve as an alternative for addressing income inequality concerns.
3. Thirdly, it investigates the reasons behind the failure of these predictions to materialize in reality.
4. Lastly, drawing from this analysis, the book aims to propose policy alternatives that can enable democracy to remain an effective solution to income inequality issues.

However, our responses to these inquiries diverge from conventional research in several significant ways. Primarily, what sets our research apart from existing studies is our intensified focus on income inequality as a product of the complex interplay between the political and economic domains, rather than a standalone examination of income inequality in isolation. Essentially, we delve deeper into the issue of income inequality and redistribution from a political economy perspective. This perspective acknowledges the crucial role played by the interaction between politics and economics, making it a central focus of our study. Our viewpoint is that income inequality and income redistribution are shaped by the institutions, policies, and laws generated by the political system, with their formation and nature being determined by the power distribution among socio-political groups. Moreover, these established institutions and policies play a role in defining the power distribution within each socio-political group. Secondly, the field of economics has primarily focused on formulating intricate policies, operating under the assumption that political challenges have already been satisfactorily addressed. However, our aim is to shift our scrutiny toward the complex and often-conflicting political dynamics underpinning redistribution: we seek to understand how policy choices are made, who the decision-makers are, and what are the motivations that drive their choices.

In alignment with these considerations, the book's structure is organized as follows:

In Chapter 2, we categorize the respective inequalities into three types: income inequality, political inequality, and opportunity inequality. We study these inequalities in both democratic and non-democratic countries and examine their worldwide trends. Additionally, we analyze the relationships between these three types of inequalities using cross-national data and modeling. Chapter 3 presents M-R's argument that democracy harbors an inherent self-correcting mechanism against income inequality. Additionally, it offers an overview of the outcomes derived from previous empirical research conducted on the M-R hypothesis. In Chapter 4, the focus shifts to elucidating why redistribution policies face challenges in yielding effective results within democratic systems. This inquiry is centered on a detailed examination of the policy development process, which emerges from the interplay between the economic and political domains. In Chapter 5, an investigation is conducted to discern the political and economic variables that have positively or negatively influenced the efficacy of income redistribution policies within democratic nations over the past three decades. This analysis involves the utilization of diverse statistical data and places specific emphasis on the findings outlined in Chapter 4. Chapter 6 presents policy alternatives and draws conclusions based on the preceding discussions.

1.2 Can democracy mitigate the rising levels of inequality?

Schattschneider (1960) argues that democracy's role is to provide the public with an alternative power system to challenge economic power. This suggests that democracy provides institutional and policy mechanisms to regulate the inequality originating from economic power, thereby protecting the political and economic interests of citizens. In economics too, building on prior research by Downs (1957) and Romer (1975), M-R propose that in a democratic system where the majority of citizens have voting rights, an increase in income inequality leads to public support for income redistribution policies. These policies can help alleviate income inequality.

However, reality presents a different perspective. In democratic countries over the past four decades, lower- and middle-class voters have struggled to effectively implement tax increases on the wealthy, even during periods of rising income inequality. Consequently, income redistribution efforts have not been successful (World Bank, 2006; World Inequality Lab, 2017). Instead, the high-earner minority has manipulated policies and market rules in their favor, utilizing their economic power to monopolize market opportunities (Stiglitz, 2012). As a result, the anticipated equalizing effects of democracy proposed by M-R have not materialized, and democracy has encountered crises. Empirical studies (Sirowy and Inkeles, 1990; Gradstein and Milanovic, 2004; Mulligan et al., 2004; Scheve and Stasavage, 2009, 2010, 2012) have also grappled with establishing a clear relationship between democracy and redistribution policies. Astonishingly, empirical evidence has even emerged contradicting the M-R model. Cross-national comparative studies have revealed the presence of the Robin Hood paradox, suggesting that countries with greater income equality are actually more successful in achieving redistribution compared to countries with higher levels of income inequality.

Consequently, existing empirical studies provide evidence that the interplay between democracy, income redistribution, and inequality is more intricate than what the M-R model assumes.

Chapter 3 examines the equalizing effects of democracy suggested by the M-R hypothesis and reviews the theories and empirical findings related to the M-R hypothesis that are currently being explored in various social science disciplines, including economics, political science, and sociology.

1.3 What are the reasons why the M-R hypothesis has not succeeded?

As shown in Figure 1.1, we propose that income inequality and income redistribution are shaped by institutions and policies, which themselves are influenced by the power distribution among social and political groups. Specifically, the selection and adoption of specific policies and institutions are determined by the relative power held by different groups. This means that the preferences of powerful groups play a significant role in shaping the selection of policies and institutions among competing alternatives. Importantly, these established institutions, policies, and outcomes of income redistribution subsequently impact the power distribution within a society.

Thus, if the power distribution presumed by the M-R hypothesis is influenced by certain factors leading to unfavorable income redistribution, adopting policies and institutions that support effective income redistribution becomes challenging. Consequently, the equalizing effect of democracy may not operate as expected.

Firstly, the M-R model assumes that voters are distributed unequally across income levels, with a leftward skew, and further posits that the majority is composed of lower-income groups. It also assumes that individuals' political preferences and policy choices are solely determined by their income levels. If these assumptions hold true, the lower-income groups would form the majority, resulting in a favorable power distribution for them in policy decisions. This advantageous power distribution enables the adoption and implementation of income redistribution policies that align with the preferences of lower-income groups.

The second assumption of the M-R model is that the political realm operates on the principle of equality, where each person has an equal vote regardless of their income level. Even in the face of increasing income inequality, this assumption posits that the principle of equality remains unaffected. In other words, the model assumes that income inequality does not translate into political inequality. The second assumption suggests that political inequality stemming from economic inequality does not occur, notwithstanding that elites attempt to enhance their political influence through their wealth, such as through lobbying or media promotion of specific ideologies. The power distribution in the political domain remains equal, adhering to the principle of one person, one vote.

The M-R model is founded on two primary assumptions, as outlined below.

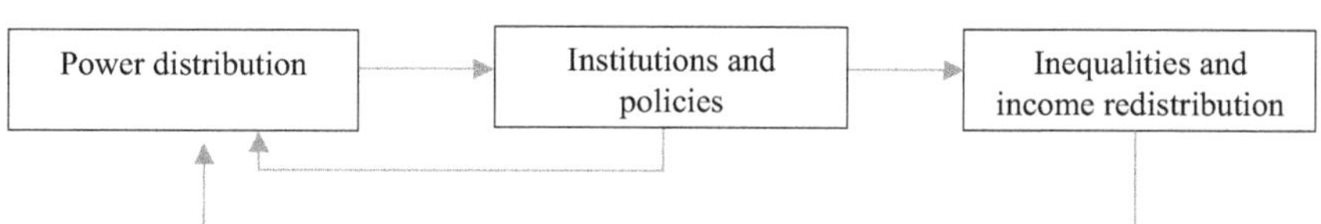

Figure 1.1 The interaction between power distribution, institutions, policies, and the outcomes of income redistribution

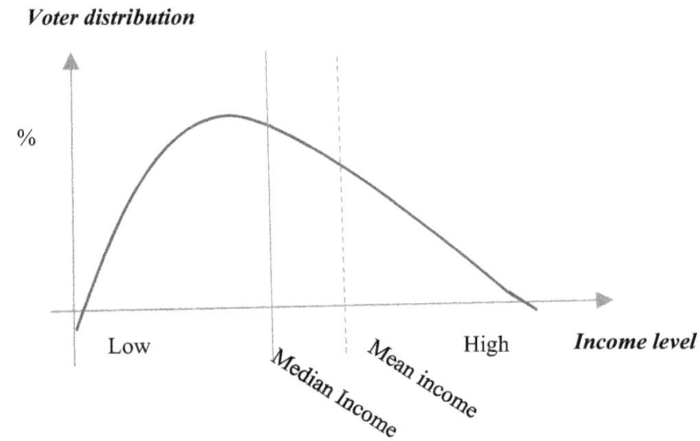

Figure 1.2 Voter distribution assumed by the M-R hypothesis

As illustrated in Figure 1.2, in line with the first assumption of the M-R model, the distribution of voters based on income level exhibits a leftward skew, indicating that the majority consists of lower-income groups. Additionally, considering that policy preferences are influenced by income levels, the distribution of voters who support income redistribution policies, represented by the ***I*** in Figure 1.3, aligns closely with the distribution shown in Figure 1.2.

However, if the two assumptions of the M-R hypothesis are not met, there is a possibility of a shift in the power distribution. In such cases, even if the majority comprises lower-income groups and income inequality increases, the implementation of income redistribution policies may not occur. Consequently, the equalizing effect of democracy may not be realized.

Firstly, deviating from the first assumption, if the policy preferences of lower-income groups are influenced not only by income levels but also by additional factors such as religion, race, ideology, expectations, and distrust of the government, the support for income redistribution policies among voters may take a different shape, resembling the ***II*** distribution in Figure 1.3 rather

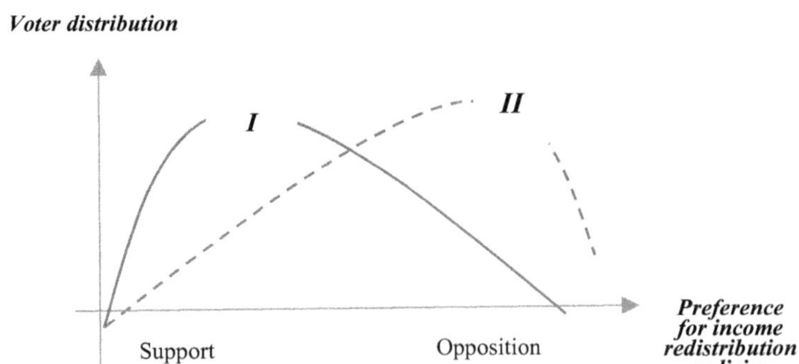

Figure 1.3 Voter distribution supporting income redistribution policies

than the ***I*** distribution. Numerous prior studies have offered explanations for this shift, including: 1) opportunistic behavior among members (Acemoglu and Robinson, 2008 and Acemoglu et al. 2013), 2) the presence of cleavages based on religious, racial, ethnic, and ideological conflicts (Schattschneider, 1960), 3) the existence of policy regimes (Przeworski, 2014), 4) high distrust of government-led income redistribution policies due to government corruption (Rothstein, 2005), and 5) an increased likelihood for low-income or middle-income groups to ascend to higher income brackets (Bénabou and Ok, 2001). Previous research has primarily focused on analyzing the theoretical and empirical reasons behind the lack of validity in the M-R hypothesis from this perspective.

Secondly, if the efforts made by elites to acquire significant *de facto* political power are successful in expanding their influence in political decision-making, representation, and political engagement, the political domain can no longer be seen as an egalitarian domain immune from the influence of wealth. The affluent class gains *de facto* political power through various means, including lobbying, campaign financing, establishing pressure groups, engaging in collective action, leveraging threats of capital flight, and mobilizing media and ideology. In such a scenario, a notable disparity arises between ***the distribution of effective political power***, which takes into account *de facto* political power (Figure 1.4), and ***the distribution of political power based solely on the number of voters*** (Figure 1.2). These shifts in the distribution of political power result in political inequality, characterized by unequal representation, limited political participation, unequal access to decision-making processes, and differential treatment by political institutions, between the wealthy class and the low-income class. Consequently, the decisive voter responsible for determining income redistribution is no longer an individual with median income but rather the affluent elite who have accumulated political power. Therefore, even if income inequality increases, it may still be difficult to achieve proper redistribution.

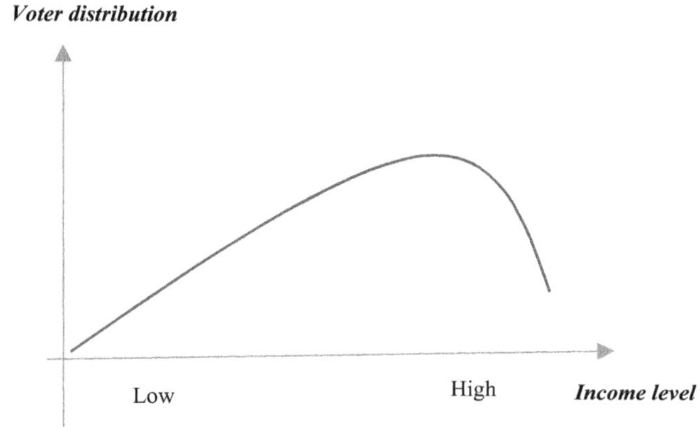

Figure 1.4 Distribution of effective political power

Thus, by relaxing either the first or second assumption, the power distribution can undergo changes that impede the adoption of income redistribution policies in a democratic system, despite an increase in income inequality. Consequently, the equalizing effect of democracy may not be realized.

> Our approach focuses on how power is distributed, as opposed to previous studies that seek to identify the reasons for the ineffectiveness of the equalizing effect of democracy. We specifically emphasize the power distribution assumed by the M-R model. By reorganizing and reinterpreting existing research findings with an emphasis on these power distribution assumptions, we aim to provide a new perspective. Additionally, we develop models and conduct empirical analyses to delve deeper into the subject.

In Chapter 4, we summarize the factors leading to the first pathway of power distribution change, namely the transition from ***I*** to ***II*** in Figure 1.3, by drawing on existing studies. We focus on the complex policy formation process that occurs as the economic and political domains interact. In particular, our aim is to offer a comprehensive explanation by establishing connections between existing studies and the process of policy formation, a process arising from the interaction between the realms of politics and economics. Furthermore, based on these research findings, we construct a model consisting of three social classes and compare various scenarios, including those related to the M-R model, captured democracy, policy regimes, corrupt government, the absence of a political party representing the interests of the lower-income class under a two-party system, and class betrayal voting driven by identity cleavages.

1.4 Can the M-R hypothesis be empirically validated? How can we confirm, through empirical analysis, that changes in power distribution impede the equalizing effects of democracy?

In Chapter 5, we address these questions by undertaking empirical research. Our primary objective is to examine the validity of the M-R hypothesis using empirical evidence. We aim to determine whether democratic systems effectively mitigate income inequality and promote income redistribution. Should our empirical analysis not support the M-R hypothesis, we will undertake further empirical analysis to investigate the reasons behind this outcome, considering various scenarios.

To conduct our analysis, we utilize data from a wide range of countries, spanning the period from 1990 to 2021. We employ various indicators and datasets to measure income inequality, such as the Standardized World Income Inequality Database (SWIID), and assess the level of democracy using established indices like Polity5, Boix, Miller and Rosato (2013), and Cheibub, Gandhi, and Vreeland (2010). Additionally, we incorporate other macro-level data from the World Bank's World Development Indicators database.

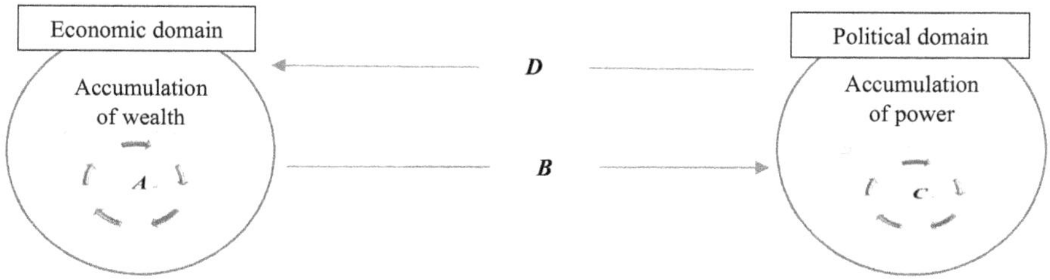

Figure 1.5 Interaction between wealth accumulation and power accumulation

Through rigorous empirical analysis, we aim to illuminate the relationships between power distribution, democracy, and the equalizing effects of income redistribution.

Figure 1.5 illustrates the interaction between the economic domain and the political domain. The economic domain ***A*** represents an exclusive space where wealth accumulation occurs, characterized by wealth concentrations that foster inequality. In contrast, the political domain ***C*** is an inclusive space where power accumulates, emphasizing inclusiveness with a focus on numbers and maximum participation. M-R optimistically expect that the political domain can rectify the uneven playing field of the economic domain through process ***D***, where the political domain intervenes in the economic domain. However, recent studies in political economy focus on process ***B***, namely, the *politics eroded by economics*. These studies scrutinize the efforts of the affluent class to convert accumulated economic wealth into political power, thereby transforming the political domain, which seeks equality, into an increasingly unequal space. On the other hand, M-R fails to grasp process ***B*** properly, overlooking that increasing inequality in the economic domain can be transferred to inequality in the political domain. Consequently, M-R optimistically predicts that democracy can easily resolve income inequality issues. However, when political inequality escalates through process ***B***, redistribution via process ***D***, i.e., *allocation of resources by politics*, becomes challenging. Moreover, if the affluent class, which has accumulated political power through process ***B***, utilize their leverage to select policies and institutions that align with their interests, this leads to cumulative inequality that further tilts the playing field in the economic domain through process ***D***.

1.5 How can we establish a "Goldilocks" balance between economic power and political power?

What measures can be taken to disrupt the cycle of economic inequality intertwining with political inequality?

The first step involves proactive measures to prevent the transformation of economic inequality into political inequality, thereby halting the spread of economic disparities into the political domain. To achieve this goal, a comprehensive set of measures must be implemented to effectively counteract the occurrence of process ***B*** in Figure 1.5. Specifically, dedicated efforts are required to reduce the influence that corporations, as embodiments of economic power in contemporary society, exert over the political landscape. More specifically, enhancing corporate transparency through governance reforms and fostering internal democratization within companies is crucial to rectify imbalances within their organizational structures. Moreover, to curb corporate influence in the political arena, limitations on the extent of financial support that corporations can provide to the political domain are necessary. Additionally, the media and academia, frequently implicated in justifying the expansion of corporate influence, should make a concerted effort to maintain their independence from such corporate sway.

Secondly, proactive efforts are required within the political domain to promote a more equitable distribution of political power. Reforms should specifically target domain ***C*** in Figure 1.5. For instance, these reforms should strive to enhance the influence of historically marginalized lower-income groups, who frequently face barriers in accessing political resources. In electoral processes, it is crucial to ensure that all candidates enjoy equal opportunities for political expression, regardless of their level of support or endorsement from wealthier segments of society. Indeed, it is crucial to empower all citizens to participate in the political process in diverse capacities, beyond their roles as mere voters. This encompasses involvement as donors, volunteers, and members of political entities. Individuals ought to have the freedom to express their political convictions without fear of repression, and the political structure should prioritize the influence of organized initiatives over financial resources, particularly regarding specific issues.

Certainly, reforms are also warranted in the electoral and party systems. To attain a more balanced power distribution within the political domain, it is vital to establish a foundation of consensus-based political systems where diverse groups and interests can actively and equally participate in the political process.

Chapter 6 contains the conclusion and summary. We present policy recommendations for the effective implementation of income redistribution in a democratic system based on the findings and analyses in this book.

Therefore, the objectives of this book are to:

i) *Examine the unexplored aspects of policy alternatives.* Often, economists either presuppose the effective resolution of complex political issues or focus exclusively on problems for which solutions already exist. Consequently, they harbor an optimistic expectation that identifying appropriate policy alternatives can readily resolve societal issues. However, our interest lies in probing the intricate and conflicting political processes that underpin the formulation of policy alternatives. Specifically, we aim to comprehend the mechanisms of policy decision-making, the actors wielding decision-making power, and the motivations driving such decisions.

ii) *Re-engage with the significant debates surrounding the M-R hypothesis.* As previously explained, the research objective of this book is not to introduce new discussions on the M-R hypothesis, but rather to systematically organize existing discussions and compare differing perspectives within a consistent analytical framework. To accomplish this, we aim to reinterpret and reorganize the discourse on M-R using the interplay between power distribution, policies, and income redistribution depicted in Figure 1.1. Additionally, we plan to analyze and compare discussions on M-R through modeling and undertake empirical research based on this groundwork.

iii) *Re-evaluate the importance of maintaining a balance between the political and economic domains.* Our objective is to explore strategies that can prevent the conversion of economic inequality into political inequality, ultimately facilitating effective income redistribution. How can we prevent the transformation of economic inequality into political inequality? How can we break the cycle that perpetuates economic and political inequality?

References

Acemoglu, D., S. Restrepo, and J. Robinson (2013), "Democracy, redistribution and inequality," *NBER Working Paper*, No. 19746.

Acemoglu, D. and J. Robinson (2008), "Persistence of power, elites, and institutions," *American Economic Review*, Vol. 98, No. 1, pp. 267–293.

American Political Science Association Task Force (2004), "American democracy in an age of rising inequality," *Perspectives on Politics*, Vol. 2, No. 4, pp. 651–666.

Bénabou, R. and E. A. Ok (2001), "Social mobility and the demand for redistribution: The POUM hypothesis," *Quarterly Journal of Economics*, Vol. 116, No. 2, pp. 447–487.

Boix, C., M. Miller, and S. Rosato (2013), "A complete data set of political regimes, 1800–2007," *Comparative Political Studies*, Vol. 46, No. 12, pp. 1523–1554.

Cheibub, J. A., J. Gandhi, and J. R. Vreeland (2010), "Democracy and dictatorship revisited," *Public Choice*, Vol. 143, No. 1/2, pp. 67–101.

Corak, M. (2013), "Income inequality, equality of opportunity, and intergenerational mobility," *Journal of Economic Perspectives*, Vol. 27, No. 3, pp. 79–102.

Downs, A. (1957), *An economic theory of democracy*, New York: Harper and Row Publishers.

Gradstein, M. and B. Milanovic (2004), "Does Liberté = Égalité? A survey of the empirical links between democracy and inequality with some evidence on the transition economies," *Journal of Economic Surveys*, Vol. 18, No. 4, pp. 515–537.

Meltzer, A. H. and S. F. Richard (1981), "A rational theory of the size of government," *Journal of Political Economy*, Vol. 89, No. 5, pp. 914–927.

Mulligan, C. B., R. Gil, and X. Sala-i-Martin (2004), "Do democracies have different public policies than nondemocracies?" *Journal of Economic Perspectives*, Vol. 18, No. 1, pp. 51–74.

Okun, A. M. (1975), *Equality and efficiency: The big trade off*, Washington, DC: Brookings Institution Press.

Ostry, J., A. Berg, and C. G. Tsangarides (2014), "Redistribution, inequality and growth," *IMF Staff Discussion Note*, SDN/14/02.

Przeworski, A. (2014), "Choices and echoes: Stability and change of policy regimes," in Magara, E. (ed), *Economic crises and policy regimes*, pp 33–55, Cheltenham: Edward Elgar.
Rawls, J. (1999), *A theory of justice*, Revised Edition, Cambridge, MA: Harvard University Press.
Romer, T. (1975), "Individual welfare, majority voting, and the properties of a linear income tax," *Journal of Public Economics*, Vol. 4, No. 2, pp. 163–185.
Rothstein, B. (2005), *Social traps and the problem of trust*, Cambridge: Cambridge University Press.
Schattschneider, E. E. (1960), *The semi-sovereign people: A realist view of democracy in America*, New York: Holt, Rinehart and Winston
Scheve, K. and D. Stasavage (2012), "Democracy, war, and wealth: Lessons from two centuries of inheritance taxation," *American Political Science Review*, Vol. 106, No. 1, pp. 82–102.
Scheve, K. and D. Stasavage (2010), "The conscription of wealth: Mass warfare and the demand for progressive taxation," *International Organization*, Vol. 64, No. 4, pp. 529–561.
Scheve, K. and D. Stasavage (2009), "Institutions, partisanship, and inequality in the long run," *World Politics*, Vol. 61, No. 2, pp. 215–253.
Sirowy, L. and A. Inkeles (1990), "The effects of democracy on economic growth and inequality: A review," *Studies in Comparative International Development*, Vol. 25, No. 1, pp. 126–157.
Stiglitz, J. E. (2012), *The price of inequality: How today's divided society endangers our future*, New York: W.W. Norton & Company.
Stockhammer, E. (2012), "Rising inequality as a root cause of the present crisis," *ERI Working Paper Series* 282.
Tridico, P. (2012), "Financial crisis and global imbalances: its labor market origins and the aftermath," *Cambridge Journal of Economics*, Vol. 36, No. 1, pp. 17–42.
World Bank (2006), *World development report 2006: Equity and development.*
World Inequality Lab (2017), *World inequality report 2018*, http://wir2018.wid.world/

2 The cumulative rise of multiple inequalities

In this chapter, we explore through modeling how income inequality, opportunity inequality, and political inequality interrelate, delineating pathways through which income inequality can precipitate political inequality and opportunity inequality, and how these resultant inequalities may subsequently amplify income inequality. Additionally, we aim to investigate whether there has been a cumulative increase in these three forms of inequality by utilizing statistical data. Thus, the primary objective of this chapter is to analyze cumulative causal relationships among various types of inequality to elucidate processes through which multiple inequalities are escalating in the world today. Secondarily, we aim to demonstrate that, contrary to the M-R hypothesis, democracy may struggle to address the problem of income inequality through the voting process if these types of inequality develop concurrently.

2.1 Trends of income inequality, political inequality, and opportunity inequality

In this section, we analyze the dynamic trends of income inequality and political inequality. By utilizing statistical data, we aim to verify whether there has been a global improvement in income inequality and political inequality since the 1980s. Moreover, we employ graphical representations to establish the connections between different forms of inequality.

2.1.1 Changes in income inequality over the past 40 years

Figures 2.1 to 2.3 present various measurements of the rise in income inequality since the 1980s. Figure 2.1 specifically illustrates the trend of the after-tax Gini index for OECD countries over the past four decades. When countries are positioned to the left of the 45-degree line, it signifies a deterioration in income distribution in 2020 compared to 1980. Conversely, positions to the right of the 45-degree line indicate that income inequality has improved over the past 40 years. With the exception of Greece, Spain, Belgium, and France, all other countries lie to the left of the 45-degree line, indicating a worsening income inequality situation in most OECD advanced economies. As of 2020,

DOI: 10.4324/9781032695754-2

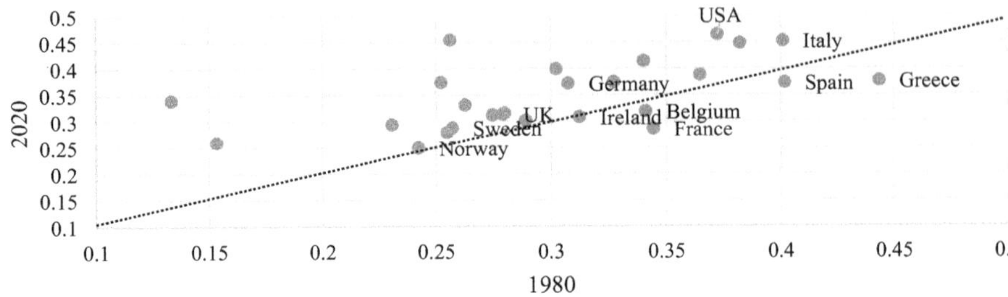

Figure 2.1 Changes in after-tax Gini index among OECD countries over the past 40 years

Source: World Inequality Database.

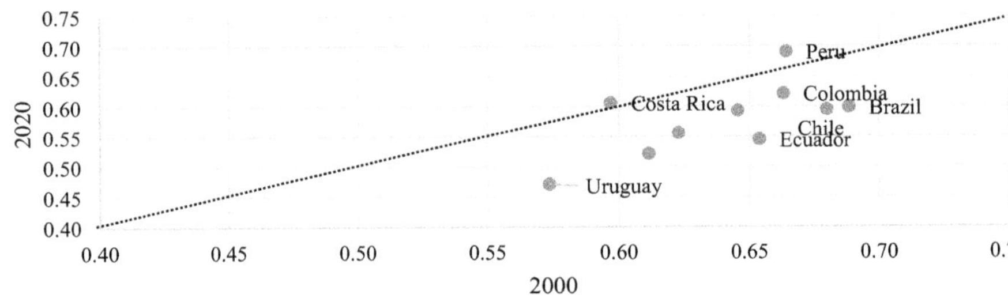

Figure 2.2 Changes in after-tax Gini index among Latin America and the Caribbean countries over the past 20 years

Source: World Inequality Database.

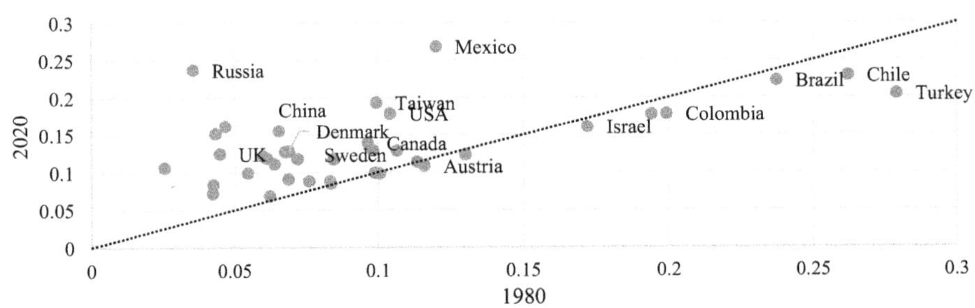

Figure 2.3 Changes in top 1% national income share over the past 40 years

Source: World Inequality Database.

the United States, Italy, Spain, and Greece exhibited higher after-tax Gini indexes compared to other countries, highlighting a more unequal income distribution in these nations. Moreover, the further the distance in the north-east direction from the 45-degree line, the more rapid the increase in income inequality between 1980 and 2020. This is clearly evidenced by the significant surge observed in the United States and Italy during that period.

Since the 1980s, income inequality has risen in the majority of countries, but South America has emerged as an exception where income inequality has actually improved over the past two decades. Figure 2.2 displays the trend of the after-tax Gini index for Central and South American countries from 2000 to 2020. Apart from Costa Rica and Peru, most countries in the region are situated to the right of the 45-degree line, in contrast to Figure 2.1. This positioning suggests that income inequality has shown improvement in the region since 2000. The success in reducing income inequality in Central and South America can be attributed to several factors, with the implementation of innovative welfare systems playing a pivotal role. These systems involve linking minimum wages to inflation and economic growth rates, as well as integrating social programs that promote human capital development and welfare, such as the Bolsa Família program. As a result of these measures, the middle class in the region has expanded substantially. Lustig et al. (2013) and ILO (2011) have identified two factors contributing to the reduction of income inequality in Latin America. They highlight the decrease in the education premium, attributed to an increased supply of highly educated workers resulting from investments in education, and underscore the role of social welfare policies, including the minimum wage.

According to Levy and Schady (2013), the decline in the skill premium due to the rise in the supply of highly educated workers accounts for 30% to 50% of the income inequality reduction in South American nations, while the expansion of pension recipients explains 5% of the decrease. Additionally, various cash transfer programs were found to explain around 25% of the change.

Figure 2.3 provides a comparison of the changes in the proportion of total income held by the top 1% over the past 40 years, using the World Inequality database. The analysis reveals that while certain countries, including some South American nations, Turkey, Israel, and Austria, experienced a decrease in the share of income held by the top 1%, the majority of OECD countries observed an increase in this measure from 1980 to 2020. As of 2020, the top 1% income share in the United States is 17.9%, in Mexico, it is 26.8%, in Russia, it is 23.8%, and in Chile, it is 22.8%. Over the analyzed period, these countries saw significant increases in the income share of their top 1%, with China experiencing a 136.8% increase, Mexico witnessing a 122.8% increase, the United States observing a 71.4% increase, and the United Kingdom seeing an 87.9% increase.

2.1.2 Changes in political inequality over the past 20 years

Upon comparing the level of income inequality with the Gini coefficient or the share of total income held by the top 1% over the past 40 years using the World Inequality Database, it was observed that income inequality has worsened in most developed countries. Conversely, although the level of income inequality remains high, it was confirmed that income inequality has decreased over the past 40 years as an exception in the case of South American countries. In this section, in addition to exploring income inequality, we also delve into the dynamic shifts of political inequality over the last 20 years, which is of particular interest to us.

Recent research has been focused on assessing the level of political inequality within societies. To achieve this, scholars have employed a comprehensive democracy dataset called Varieties of Democracy (hereafter V-Dem), which relies on expert ratings from various countries (Cole, 2018; Houle, 2018; Choi, 2021). One of the political inequality indices, known as *pi-1*, is derived from the V-Dem data set. Within V-Dem, there is a survey specifically designed to gauge *power distribution by socio-economic position*, which aligns with the objectives of this research. In this survey, country experts use a 0–4 scale to evaluate the extent to which political influence is equally distributed among the rich, middle class, and poor in a given society. The highest score, 4, indicates that political influence is equally distributed, regardless of wealth. For this study, the inequality values were calculated by normalizing and reversing the V-Dem indicator to a 100–0 scale, as described by Choi (2021). Thus, values closer to 100 signify higher levels of political inequality.

In addition to *pi-1*, another political inequality index, referred to as *pi-2*, was introduced by Choi (2021). Unlike *pi-1*, *pi-2* takes into account multiple dimensions of political power distribution, including socio-economic position, social group, and gender, as presented individually in the V-Dem dataset. Consequently, *pi-2* values reveal whether political inequality is influenced not only by wealth but also by factors such as race, religion, language, ethnicity, region, and gender. To calculate the *pi-2* values, the geometric mean of the three-point estimates of the V-Dem indicators was used. Similar to *pi-1*, the *pi-2* values were also normalized and reversed to a 100–0 scale to indicate the degree of political inequality.

Out of the 38 OECD countries, data from 36 of them were used to assess the level of political inequality between 2000 and 2020. The results, measured as *pi-1* and *pi-2*, revealed that in the case of *pi-1* (Figure 2.4), political inequality increased in 23 out of the 36 countries. Conversely, when measured as *pi-2* (Figure 2.5), political inequality increased in 18 out of the 36 countries.

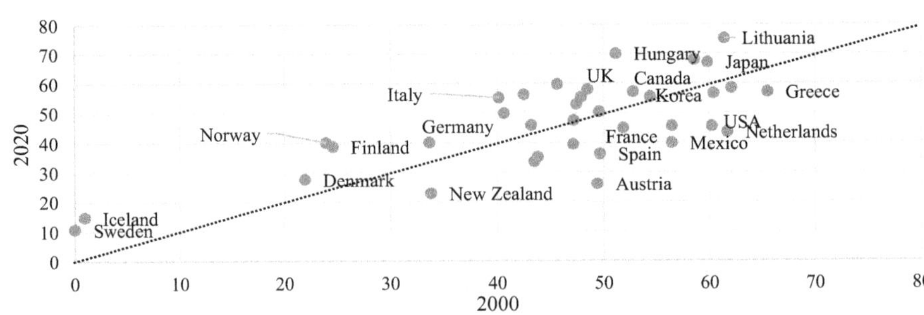

Figure 2.4 Political inequality index of OECD countries: *pi-1*

Source: V-Dem database.

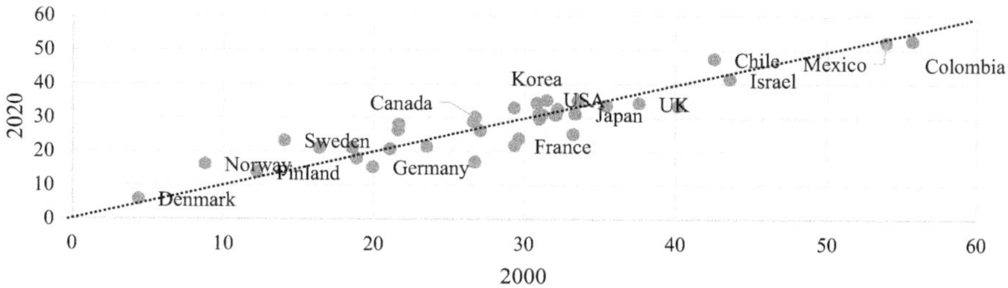

Figure 2.5 Political inequality index of OECD countries: *pi-2*

Source: V-Dem database.

Taking a closer look at *pi-1*, which gauges political inequality based on political participation and representation, it was found that Lithuania, Japan, Canada, South Korea, the United Kingdom, the Czech Republic, and Hungary all demonstrated high levels of inequality in both 2000 and 2020, and this inequality further increased over the 20-year period. In contrast, the United States, the Netherlands, and Austria, which had high inequality in 2000, experienced significant reductions in political inequality. Additionally, in the case of Nordic countries, political inequality increased over the past 20 years, but it still remained at a low level. The trends observed in pi-1 over the last two decades provide evidence in favor of the *captured democracy hypothesis*, indicating a rise in the political influence of the affluent class.

According to *pi-2*, which assesses the impact of factors like wealth, race, ethnicity, region, and gender on political inequality, countries like Colombia, Chile, Mexico, and Israel exhibited high values, indicating a greater level of political inequality in these nations. On the other hand, Nordic countries had lower levels of political inequality when measured by *pi-2* compared to other countries, but it was observed to have increased over the past 20 years. In contrast, countries such as France, Germany, and the United Kingdom showed a decline in political inequality.

2.1.3 Concurrent rise of multiple inequalities

In the preceding section, we analyzed the individual trajectories of income inequality and political inequality over time by utilizing data from the World Inequality Database and the Varieties of Democracy database. However, the focus now shifts in this section to explore the interrelation among income inequality, political inequality, and inequality of opportunity through visual representation. Here, instead of relying on the World Inequality Database and the Varieties of Democracy database as in the previous section, we employ data provided by Ferreira and Peragine (2015) concerning inequality of opportunity, income inequality, and political inequality. The rationale behind utilizing these data lies in their ability to quantify the extent of inequality of opportunity in each country using a standardized criterion.

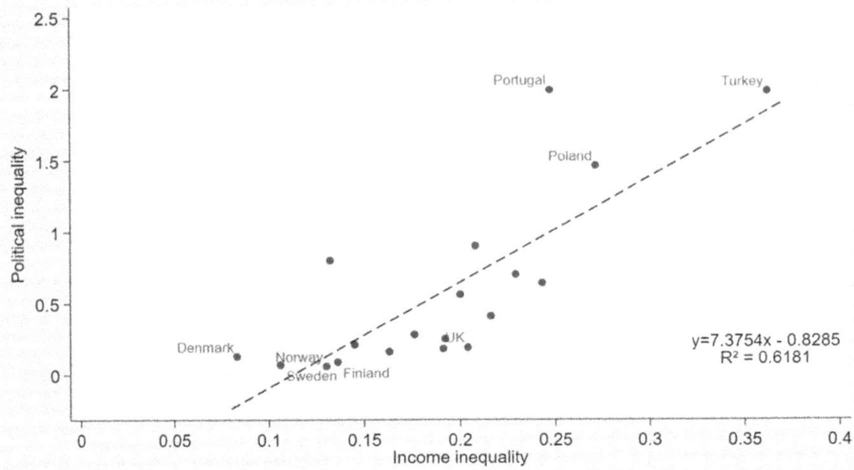

Figure 2.6 Relationship between income inequality and political inequality

Note: Lower income inequality and political inequality values signify higher levels of equality. Income inequality is gauged using the Theil-T index. The following countries are included: Belgium, Czech Republic, Denmark, Estonia, Finland, France, Germany, Greece, Hungary, Latvia, Netherlands, Norway, Poland, Portugal, Slovenia, Spain, Sweden, Turkey, UK.

Source: The income inequality index is based on Ferreira and Peragine (2015), and the political inequality data is from Dubrow (2010).

In Figure 2.6, countries are plotted along two axes. The horizontal axis represents income inequality based on the Theil-T index proposed by Ferreira and Peragine (2015). The vertical axis measures political inequality proposed by Dubrow (2010). Dubrow's study examines political inequality in Europe and does not include values for the United States and elsewhere. Therefore, the dataset is limited to the 19 European countries for which political inequality values are available. In countries such as Denmark, Finland, Norway, and Sweden, both political inequality and income inequality are low. Conversely, in Turkey, Poland, and Portugal, both political inequality and income inequality are high. Norway has the lowest political inequality (0.06), while Turkey (1.98) exhibits 33 times more political inequality than Norway. In a simple regression, the coefficient of estimation is positive and $R^2$is 0.618, indicating a high correlation between political inequality and income inequality.

OECD (2011) and Corak (2013) examine the interaction between income inequality and inequality of opportunity, while Acemoglu et al. (2013) focus on the interrelationship between income inequality and political inequality. Rawls cautions that once income inequality surpasses a certain threshold level, the influence of family background begins to rise, threatening equality of opportunity—the foundation of social justice. Recent studies (Bailey and Dynarski, 2011; OECD, 2011; Corak, 2013) have corroborated Rawls' warning by discovering that increasing income inequality leads to an even higher

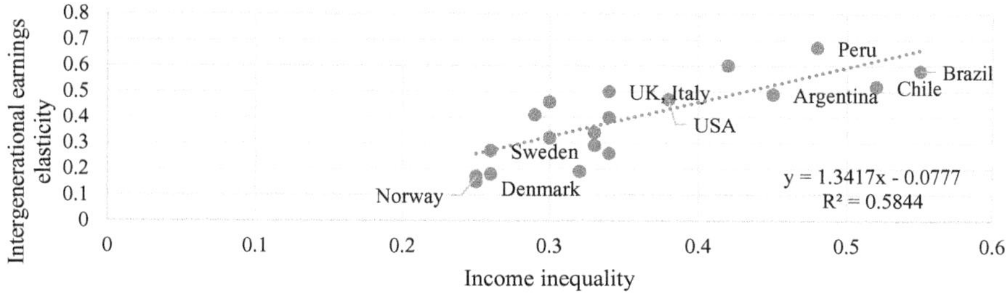

Figure 2.7 The Great Gatsby Curve: More inequality is associated with less intergenerational mobility

Note: Income inequality is measured using the Gini coefficient based on earnings after taxes and transfers. Intergenerational earnings elasticity is the elasticity between parent earnings and a son's adult earnings. The following countries are included: Peru, China, Brazil, Chile, UK, Italy, Argentina, US, Switzerland, Pakistan, France, Spain, Japan, Germany, New Zealand, Sweden, Australia, Canada, Finland, Norway, Denmark.

Source: Corak (2013) and OECD (2011).

influence of family background and parental income on the expected earnings of children relative to those children's own efforts. These studies also demonstrate that the increase in inequality of opportunity further exacerbates income inequality and negatively impacts economic growth. The OECD (2011) finds that in countries with high income inequality (Italy, Britain, and the United States), social mobility is low, while in northern Europe, where income inequality is low, social mobility is high and children's income is less affected by family background. Corak (2013) presents similar findings based on OECD studies. Using *The Great Gatsby Curve* (Figure 2.7), Corak finds that the more unequal the income distribution is in a parent generation, the higher the influence of parental income on child income. In the UK, USA, and Italy, where income inequality is high, parental income has a strong influence on child income. In these countries, the elasticity of child income to parent income is approximately 0.5, while in northern Europe it is 0.2. This implies that, in the UK, USA, and Italy, approximately 50% of any parental advantage or disadvantage is transferred from parent to child, while less than one-fifth is transferred in the Nordic countries. In a similar context, Bailey and Dynarski (2011) performed an empirical analysis of American society, controlling for cognitive ability. They discovered that for those born in the 1980s, a generation characterized by relatively high income inequality, the income level of one's parents was a stronger determinant of whether one attended college than it was for those born in the relatively income-equal 1960s.

Figure 2.8, illustrating the relationship between income inequality and inequality of opportunity, is constructed using data from 41 countries provided by Ferreira and Peragine (2015). The horizontal axis represents income inequality as measured by the Theil-T index. The vertical axis measures inequality of opportunity. Both inequality of opportunity and income inequality are low in the Nordic countries of Denmark, Finland, Norway, and Sweden.

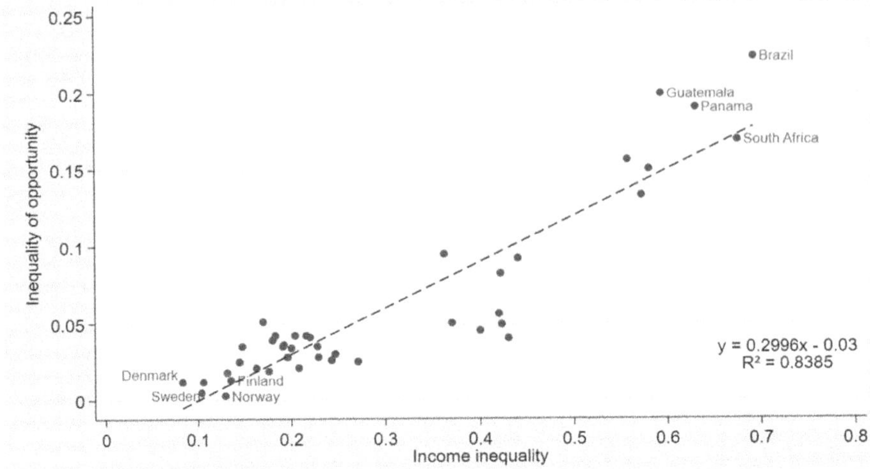

Figure 2.8 Relationship between income inequality and inequality of opportunity

Note: Lower income inequality and political inequality values signify higher levels of equality. Income inequality is gauged using the Theil-T index. The following countries are included: Austria, Belgium, Brazil, Colombia, Cyprus, Czech Republic, Denmark, Ecuador, Egypt, Estonia, Finland, France, Germany, Ghana, Greece, Guatemala, Guinea, Hungary, India, Ireland, Italy, Ivory Coast, Latvia, Lithuania, Luxembourg, Madagascar, Netherlands, Norway, Panama, Peru, Poland, Portugal, Slovakia, Slovenia, South Africa, Spain, Sweden, Turkey, Uganda, UK, USA.

Source: The data is sourced from Ferreira and Peragine (2015).

Conversely, Brazil, Guatemala, Panama, and South Africa exhibit both high inequality of opportunity and high income inequality. Denmark has the lowest opportunity inequality at 0.012, whereas inequality of opportunity in Italy is 0.028, in the UK is 0.042, and in the USA is 0.0409. Thus, countries with high intergenerational earnings elasticities under *The Great Gatsby Curve* also display high inequality of opportunity. A simple regression analysis of income inequality and inequality of opportunity yields a positive estimated coefficient, with a R^2 value of 0.838. This suggests that the two inequalities are highly and positively correlated.

Figure 2.9 illustrates how inequality of opportunity contributes to income inequality. In Guatemala, the contribution of opportunity inequality to income inequality is the highest at 33.56%, followed by Brazil at 32.23%. The United Kingdom and the United States also show high rates: 20.59% and 18.6%, respectively. Norway, on the other hand, is the lowest, at 2.31%.

2.2 Cumulative relationship among multiple inequalities

As demonstrated above using statistical data, we observed a widespread increase in both income inequality and political inequality across numerous countries over recent decades. Moreover, we noted a simultaneous rise in income inequality, political inequality, and inequality of opportunity. In this

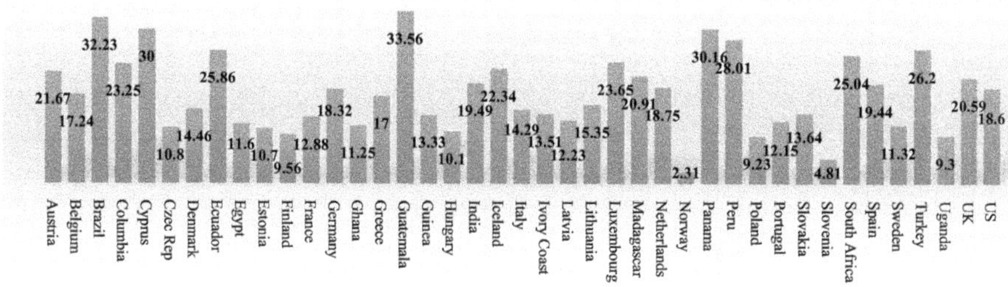

Figure 2.9 Contribution of inequality of opportunity to income inequality (%)

Note: Please refer to Appendix 1 for an explanation of the estimation method.

Source: The data is sourced from Ferreira and Peragine (2015).

section, we clarify the cumulative progression of income inequality, political inequality, and opportunity inequality by reviewing and modeling existing research findings.

Research on political inequality and inequality of opportunity provides insights into the concurrent rise of diverse socio-political inequalities, beyond merely income inequality. Utilizing Figure 2.10, we can elucidate the cumulative increase or co-occurrence of these inequalities as follows: The wealthy class strives to enhance their *de facto* political power (Path ① in Figure 2.10) to pursue policies and resource distribution that favor their own interests. Through this, they aim to exert influence over political power and government decision-making, primarily concerning equality of opportunity. An example highlighted by Corak (2013) involves the influence exerted by affluent parents to allocate public resources toward schools and educational institutions where their children predominantly enroll. In the case of France, a similar situation arises where educational resources are focused on *Grandes Écoles*, institutions attended by children from affluent families, rather than universities, which are more commonly attended by children from working-class backgrounds (Piketty, 2014). Another example pertains to wealthy individuals who seek to shape favorable changes in inheritance or gift tax-related policies that benefit themselves. They employ various lobbying strategies, shape public opinion in their

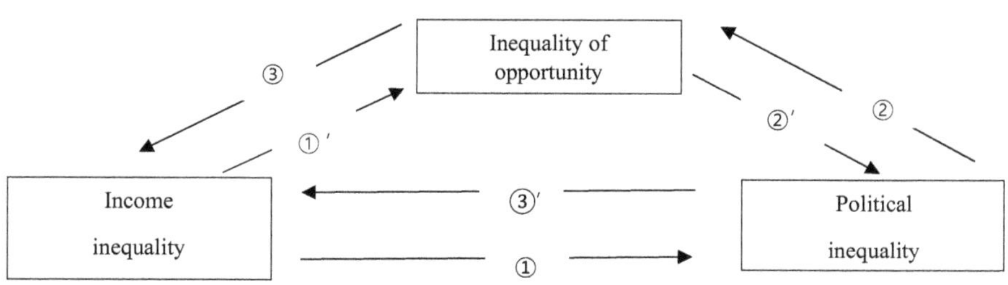

Figure 2.10 Cumulative rise of multiple inequalities

favor, and may even use the threat of capital flight. According to Piketty and Saez (2007), the United States witnessed a significant reduction in the average federal tax rate for the top 1% during the mid-2000s, amounting to approximately one-third of its level in the 1970s. Additionally, the maximum inheritance tax rate, which had peaked at around 70% in the early 1970s, has steadily declined since the mid-1970s. Specifically, the Bush administration actively pursued the elimination of the inheritance tax, citing the belief that lower tax rates stimulate economic growth. Although the inheritance tax resurfaced after the global financial crisis, it was essentially abolished during the Bush administration. In a similar vein, the demand by Korean conglomerates to abolish inheritance and gift taxes, using the justification of promoting investment activation, can be understood within the same context. Changes in inheritance tax policies, influenced by political inequality, pose challenges in ensuring equal opportunities at the starting line, as emphasized by Rawls (Path ② in Figure 2.10). Consequently, the disparities arising from differences in family backgrounds perpetuate and exacerbate economic inequality (Path ③ in Figure 2.10). According to Corak (2013), variations in family background have a significant impact on the income levels of children. This phenomenon is known as the intergenerational transmission of poverty. In the United States, when parents belong to the highest income bracket, over 50% of their children do not experience a decline in their income below the top 20% bracket. Conversely, when parents belong to the lowest income bracket, over 50% of their children remain within the bottom 30% income bracket. Canada also demonstrates a comparable pattern, albeit to a lesser degree than the United States. As economic inequality widens, the impoverished segment of the population faces a decrease in their ability to allocate financial resources toward their children's education. Consequently, this poses difficulties for individuals with comparable talents and abilities, as outlined by Rawls, in achieving comparable opportunities and fulfilling their expectations in life (Path ①' in Figure 2.10). When comparing the education expenses of children from the top 20% income bracket and the bottom 20% income bracket in the United States, significant disparities become evident. In the 1970s, the lower-income bracket spent $835, which increased to $1,300 in the mid-2000s. In contrast, the upper-income bracket spent $3,500 in the mid-1970s, but this amount rose to $9,000 in the mid-2000s (Corak, 2013). Over a span of 30 years, while education expenditures for children in the lower-income bracket increased by $500, the upper class experienced an increase of $5,500, representing eleven times more. Stiglitz (2012) made a similar observation, shedding light on the composition of students in prestigious US universities. It was found that 74% of students come from the top 25% income bracket, whereas only 9% come from the bottom 50% income bracket, emphasizing the significant disparity. Similarly, according to Piketty (2014), the average annual income of parents of Harvard University students amounts to $450,000, placing them within the top 2% income level in the United States.

If there is a disparity in educational opportunities based on social class stemming from increasing income inequality, individuals who are marginalized from accessing education also find themselves marginalized from participating in political decision-making processes. This is primarily due to their limited social networks and the inability to effectively convey their viewpoints within policy-making systems, making it challenging for them to influence policy decisions (Path ②' in Figure 2.10). Consequently, affluent individuals possessing the capability to effectively influence political decision-making and possessing stronger social networks can drive institutional changes that align with their own interests, thereby intensifying the concentration of economic power (Path ③' in Figure 2.10).

2.3 Model

In this section, we conduct a comprehensive analysis of the research outcomes presented in Figure 2.10 using modeling methodologies.

2.3.1 Demographics, preferences, and human capital accumulation

We adapt the Solon (2004) model to analyze the cumulative relationships between income inequality, opportunity inequality, and political inequality. For simplicity, we make the following assumptions.

1. The population of a society is fixed and normalized at 1.
2. i represents class, and there are two classes (or groups) in a society:[1] the elite class (h) and the ordinary-citizen class (l). Defined by income level, the elite class is the high-income class (or the wealthy) and the ordinary-citizen class encompasses both lower-income and middle-income citizens.
3. The ordinary-citizen class significantly outnumbers the elite class. If the population weight of the elite class is $\varnothing$, then that of the ordinary-citizen class is $1\text{-}\varnothing$. This implies that $\varnothing < \frac{1}{2}$ and $\varnothing$ is fixed. Regardless of the political regime, the elite class and ordinary-citizen class are defined as the only two groups constituting the population.
4. Members of each class share the same preferences and income.
5. Each family consists of one parent of generation t and one child of generation $t + 1$.

We assume the Cobb-Douglas utility function for the representative parent of class i,

$$U_{i,t} = (1-\alpha)\log C_{i,t} + \alpha log \Upsilon_{i,t+1} \tag{2.1}$$

where $i \in \{h, l\}$.

We presume that the parent is content with his or her own consumption ($C_{i,t}$) and with the child's lifetime income ($\Upsilon_{i,t+1}$). α is a parameter indicating the degree of altruism of the parent, with a value between 0 and 1. The closer this value is to 1, the more altruistic the parent is deemed to be. We also assume that α and $1 - \alpha$ are the same for each class.

Equation 2.2 represents a representative parent's budget constraint,

$$(1-\tau)\Upsilon_{i,t} = C_{i,t} + I_{i,t} + L_{i,t} \tag{2.2}$$

where τ signifies the tax rate, which is the same for each class.

We assume that the government solely spends tax revenue on education subsidies for households, implying that education subsidies function as income redistribution. A representative parent of class i allocates his or her disposable income ($(1 - \tau)\Upsilon_{i,t}$) to the parent's own consumption ($C_{i,t}$), investment in the child's education ($I_{i,t}$), and expenditures for the acquisition of *de facto* political power ($L_{i,t}$). Investing in the acquisition of *de facto* political power entails spending on activities (lobbying and political donations) that contribute to the expansion of *de facto* political power of the respective class. These investments also encompass maintenance costs of the organizations (associations and labor unions) that represent the respective class interests.

We assume that a representative parent of class i invests a certain percentage (β_i) of his or her disposable income in the acquisition of *de facto* political power.

$$L_{i,t} = \beta_i(1-\tau)\Upsilon_{i,t} \tag{2.3}$$

The expected earnings ($\Upsilon_{i,t+1}$) of a representative parent's child at time $t + 1$ is determined by the level of human capital at time $t + 1$.

$$\log \Upsilon_{i,t+1} = \mu_i + p\pi_{i,t+1} \tag{2.4}$$

In equation 2.4, π and p represent the levels of human capital and earnings return to human capital, respectively. μ_i signifies other sources of income, such as asset income, and is assumed to be fixed.

Equation 2.5 represents the accumulation of human capital. The human capital of class i's children is accumulated both through education and on-the-job training. The accumulation of human capital through education is determined by parental investment in the education of the children ($I_{i,t}$) and government education subsidies to class i's children ($GV_{i,t}$). Additionally, we assume that the human capital accumulated through on-the-job training ($\bar{e}_i$) is fixed from generation to generation. θ and η represent the marginal products of human capital investment ($I_{i,t}$ and $GV_{i,t}$), and of knowledge and experience formed through on-the-job training, respectively,

$$\pi_{i,t+1} = \theta log\left(I_{i,t} + GV_{i,t}\right) + \eta\bar{e}_i \tag{2.5}$$

where θ, η and $\bar{e}_i > 0$.

Parents in the elite class, with higher incomes, can invest in their children's education at a higher level than can members of the ordinary-citizen class. Therefore, $I_{h,t} > I_{l,t}$ is assumed. However, the allocation by the government of education subsidies to each class is determined by the respective political powers of the classes. If the political power of the elite class surpasses that of the ordinary-citizen class, the interests of the elite class will be more strongly reflected in the allocation of education subsidies. Consequently, subsidies will be more concentrated on children of the elite class. On the other hand, if the political power of the ordinary-citizen class surpasses that of the elite class, ordinary citizens will dictate the allocation of education subsidies and will allocate more of these funds to their own children.[2]

If the political power of the elite class ($PO_{h,t}$) is greater than the political power of the ordinary-citizen class ($PO_{l,t}$)—that is, if $PO_{h,t} - PO_{l,t} > 0$—then the education subsidies per elite-class child ($GV_{h,t}$) will be greater than the tax paid by elite-class parents ($\tau Y_{h,t}$). Equation 2.6 represents the government education subsidies per elite-class child,

$$GV_{h,t} = \left(\delta_h \tau Y_{h,t}\right) \tag{2.6}$$

where $\delta_h > 0$.

In equation 2.6, if the power of the elite class is higher than that of the ordinary-citizen class, elite families will receive education subsidies in excess of tax paid by the elite class, so that $\delta_h > 1$. Thus, through education subsidies, income is redistributed from the ordinary-citizen class to the elite class. Equation 2.7 represents government education subsidies per ordinary citizen–class child,

$$GV_{l,t} = \left(\delta_l \tau Y_{l,t}\right) \tag{2.7}$$

where $\delta_l > 0$.

Conversely, if the political power of the ordinary-citizen class dominates the political power of the elite class ($PO_{h,t} - PO_{l,t} < 0$), the ordinary-citizen class in equation 2.7 will receive education subsidies in excess of ordinary citizen-class taxes paid ($\delta_l > 1$). In this case, the elite class will not receive as much in subsidies as elite-class taxes paid, so that $\delta_h < 1$.

Equation 2.8 represents the government budget constraint. The government spends collected taxes solely on education subsidies.

$$\varnothing \tau Y_{h,t} + \left(1 - \varnothing\right) \tau Y_{l,t} = \varnothing \delta_h \tau Y_{h,t} + \left(1 - \varnothing\right) \delta_l \tau Y_{l,t} \tag{2.8}$$

The left side of equation 2.8 represents the government budget, while education subsidies are denoted on the right side.

2.3.2 Political power

The political power[3] of each class is determined by two factors. The first factor is the number of group members. Under democracy, the number of group members is a more critical factor in determining political power than it is under authoritarianism due to the principle of majority rule. The second determining factor is the total investment by class *i* in *de facto* political power acquisition ($D_{i,t}$).

Based on this assumption, equation 2.9 represents the function of political power of the ordinary-citizen class, having *1-∅* members,

$$PO_{l,t} = \log\left(n_l\left(1-\varnothing\right)\right)^{\gamma} D_{l,t}^{1-\gamma} \tag{2.9}$$

where $0 < n_l \leq 1$ *and* $0 \leq \gamma \leq 1$.

In equation 2.9, γ represents the degree of democratization of the society. The closer γ is to 1, the more political power is determined based on the principle of majority rule. Conversely, the closer γ is to 0, the more the political power of classes is determined by their *de facto* political power. Thus, under an authoritarian government, this value is close to zero. However, in a more democratic state, γ would approach 1, making investment in *de facto* political power less efficient.

There is a difference between the number of members in the ordinary-citizen class (*1-∅*) and the number of ordinary citizen–class members who actually exercise their right to vote ($n_l(1-\varnothing)$). Numerous prior studies identify factors contributing to this discrepancy: i) opportunistic behavior among members (Acemoglu and Robinson, 2008), ii) low voter turnout due to high illiteracy rates and economic hardship (American Political Science Association Task Force, 2004),[4] iii) the presence of cleavages based on religious, racial, ethnic, and ideological conflict (Schattschneider, 1960), iv) the existence of a policy regime (Przeworski, 2014), and v) high distrust of government-led income redistribution policies due to government corruption (Rothstein, 2005). This implies that the number of ordinary citizen-class members who actually vote for the interests of the ordinary-citizen class may not reach 1-∅; rather, in the presence of the above factors, this number will be less than 1-∅.[5] In equation 2.9, n_l represents the percentage of citizens actually voting for the interests of the ordinary-citizen class. If all ordinary citizens vote for the interests of the ordinary-citizen class, the equation is $n_l = 1$.

Total investment by ordinary citizens in *de facto* political power ($D_{l,t}$) is derived from equation 2.3 as follows:

$$D_{l,t} = n_l\left(1-\varnothing\right)L_{l,t} = n_l\left(1-\varnothing\right)\beta_l\left(1-\tau\right)\Upsilon_{l,t} \tag{2.10}$$

As previously explained, equation 2.9 differentiates between the number of class members actually exercising their right to vote and the total number of members. Conversely, equation 2.10 distinguishes between the number of ordinary citizen-class members investing in *de facto* power ($n_l(1 - \varnothing)$) and the total number of ordinary citizen-class members ($1 - \varnothing$). Therefore, equation 2.10 assumes that those who vote for the interests of the ordinary-citizen class also invest to obtain ordinary citizen-class *de facto* political power.

Consequently, equation 2.9 can be expressed as follows:

$$PO_{l,t} = \log\left(n_l\left(1-\varnothing\right)\right)^{\gamma}\left(n_l\left(1-\varnothing\right)\beta_l\left(1-\tau\right)\Upsilon_{l,t}\right)^{1-\gamma} \tag{2.11}$$

Similarly, the level of political power of the elite class can be expressed as follows,

$$PO_{h,t} = \log\left(n_h\varnothing\right)^{\gamma}\left(n_h\varnothing\beta_h\left(1-\tau\right)\Upsilon_{h,t}\right)^{1-\gamma} \tag{2.12}$$

where $0 < n_h \leq 1$.

Equations 2.11 and (2.12) demonstrate that if a large number of ordinary citizens do not exercise their right to vote ($n_l < n_h$) for the five reasons described above, a relatively small number of elites actively participating in an election may be able to form a voting majority.

Equation 2.13 combines equations 2.11 and 2.12 to calculate the difference in power between the two classes.

$$PO_{h,t} - PO_{l,t} = \log\left(\frac{n_h\varnothing}{n_l\left(1-\varnothing\right)}\right)\left(\frac{\beta_h}{\beta_l}\right)^{1-\gamma} + \log\left(\frac{\Upsilon_{h,t}}{\Upsilon_{l,t}}\right)^{1-\gamma} \tag{2.13}$$

We then derive the following:

$$\log\left(\frac{n_h\varnothing}{n_l\left(1-\varnothing\right)}\right)\left(\frac{\beta_h}{\beta_l}\right)^{1-\gamma} = c_0 \; and \log\frac{\Upsilon_{h,t}}{\Upsilon_{l,t}} = G_t \tag{2.14}$$

In equation 2.14, G_t represents the income gap between the elite class and the ordinary-citizen class in period t, the income gap being the level of income inequality in the parent generation.[6]

Equation 2.13 can be expressed as follows:

$$PO_{h,t} - PO_{l,t} = c_0 + \left(1-\gamma\right)G_t \tag{2.15}$$

As indicated in equations 2.14 and 2.15, the greater the values of n_h, $1 - \gamma$, β_h, $\varnothing$ *and* G_t, the wider will be the political power gap ($P_{h,t} - P_{l,t}$). Conversely, the greater values of γ, n_p, $(1 - \phi)$ *and* β_p the smaller the political power gap will be between the elite and ordinary-citizen classes and the more relative political power the ordinary-citizen class will hold.

As demonstrated in equations 2.6, 2.7, and 2.13, income inequality influences investment in *de facto* political power and this eventually leads to more inequality of political power. Moreover, the expanding political power gap between the two classes affects decision-making on the allocation of education subsidies, which further exacerbates the uneven distribution of human capital (equation 2.5). As seen in equations 2.4 and 2.5, an uneven distribution of accumulated human capital can even affect income inequality in the next generation.

2.3.3 *Cumulative relationship between income inequality, inequality of opportunity, and political inequality*

Given equations 2.2 through 2.5, maximizing the utility function of a representative parent (equation 2.1) under budget constraints (equation 2.2) yields an optimal level of human capital investment in the representative child (I^*), as shown in equations 2.16 through 2.18.

In equation 2.16, which describes the utility function of a representative parent of the elite class, κ and λ indicate the return on investment on human capital accumulated through education and the return on investment on human capital accumulated through on-the-job training, respectively,

$$U_{h,t} = (1-\alpha)\log\left((1-\tau)(1-\beta_h)Y_{h,t} - I_{h,t}\right) + \alpha\mu_h + \alpha\kappa\log\left(I_{h,t} + GV_{h,t}\right) + \alpha\lambda\bar{e}_h \qquad (2.16)$$

where $\kappa = p\theta$ *and* $\lambda = \eta p$.

Estebez-Abe et al. (2001) find that the return on investment (κ) on human capital accumulated through education (i.e., wage premium from tertiary education) is higher in production systems operating on general technology than in production systems based on firm- or industry-specific technologies. This is because human capital accumulated through education can be applied to a wider range of industries and areas in general-technology production systems. Conversely, in firm- or industry-specific production systems, the educational wage premium is relatively low, while the return on investment in human capital accumulated through on-the-job training (λ) is higher. For instance, wage premiums from tertiary education are higher in the United States, which excels in general technology, compared to other countries. This is in contrast to countries such as Germany and Denmark, where firm- or industry-specific technologies are deemed more valuable and the education premium is relatively low. Therefore, the value of κ, which represents the educational wage premium, varies from country to country depending on the mix of production systems.

The first-order condition for maximizing utility is as follows:

$$\frac{\partial U_{h,t}}{\partial I_{h,t}} = \frac{-(1-\alpha)}{(1-\tau)(1-\beta_h)\Upsilon_{h,t} - I_{h,t}} + \frac{\alpha\kappa}{(I_{h,t} + GV_{h,t})} = 0 \tag{2.17}$$

Solving for the optimal choice of $I_{h,t}$ yields the following:

$$I^*_{h,t} = \frac{\alpha\kappa}{1-\alpha(1-\kappa)}(1-\tau)(1-\beta_h)\Upsilon_{h,t} + \frac{(1-\alpha)}{1-\alpha(1-\kappa)}GV_{h,t} \tag{2.18}$$

From equations 2.4, 2.5, 2.6, 2.18, the income transmission equation for the elite class is as follows:

$$\log \Upsilon_{h,t+1} = \kappa log \Upsilon_{h,t} + \kappa log \frac{\alpha\kappa(1-\tau)(1-\beta_h) + \delta_h\tau(2(1-\alpha)+\alpha\kappa)}{1-\alpha(1-\kappa)} + \lambda\bar{e}_h + \mu_h \tag{2.19}$$

Similarly, the income transmission equation of the ordinary-citizen class is as follows:

$$\log \Upsilon_{l,t+1} = \kappa log \Upsilon_{l,t} + \kappa log \frac{\alpha\kappa(1-\tau)(1-\beta_l) + \delta_l\tau(2(1-\alpha)+\alpha\kappa)}{1-\alpha(1-\kappa)} + \lambda\bar{e}_l + \mu_l \tag{2.20}$$

Subtracting equation 2.20 from equation 2.19 yields equation 2.21 as follows:

$$\begin{aligned}\log \Upsilon_{h,t+1} - \log \Upsilon_{l,t+1} &= \kappa(\log \Upsilon_{h,t} - \log \Upsilon_{l,t}) \\ &+\kappa log \frac{\alpha\kappa(1-\tau)(1-\beta_h) + \delta_h\tau(2(1-\alpha)+\alpha\kappa)}{\alpha\kappa(1-\tau)(1-\beta_l) + \delta_l\tau(2(1-\alpha)+\alpha\kappa)} \\ &+\lambda(\bar{e}_h - \bar{e}_l) + (\mu_h - \mu_l)\end{aligned} \tag{2.21}$$

Next, we make the following assumption:

$$\begin{aligned}\log \Upsilon_{h,t+1} - \log \Upsilon_{l,t+1} &= G_{t+1} \;\&\; log \Upsilon_{h,t} - \log \Upsilon_{l,t} = G_t \text{ and} \\ &\kappa \log \frac{\alpha\kappa(1-\tau)(1-\beta_h) + \delta_h\tau(2(1-\alpha)+\alpha\kappa)}{\alpha\kappa(1-\tau)(1-\beta_l) + \delta_l\tau(2(1-\alpha)+\alpha\kappa)} \\ &+\lambda(\bar{e}_h - \bar{e}_l) + (\mu_h - \mu_l) = f_0\end{aligned}$$

Thus, equation 2.21 is expressed as follows:

$$\Delta G = G_{t+1} - G_t = (\kappa - 1)G_t + f_0 \tag{2.22}$$

Equation 2.22 implies that the extent to which the child generation can reduce the income gap (or income inequality) relative to the parent generation ($\Delta G <> 0$) is determined by the income gap in the parent generation (G_t), the return on investment on human capital (k), and the value of f_0.

Figure 2.11 illustrates four scenarios where the income gap between the elite and ordinary-citizen classes in the child generation varies based on the values of κ, f_0 and G_t.

In Case 1, the larger the income gap in the parent generation, the greater the income gap in the child generation. This is because, if the return on investment on human capital accumulated through education ($\kappa > 1$) is sufficiently high, the income gap in the parent generation leads to a disparity in educational expenditure for children. Due to the high return on investment in education, high-income elites are likely to invest more in their children's education, and this substantial investment in education further exacerbates the income gap in the child generation. Additionally, since f_0 is positive in Case 1, the relative weight of investment by elite parents in their children's education

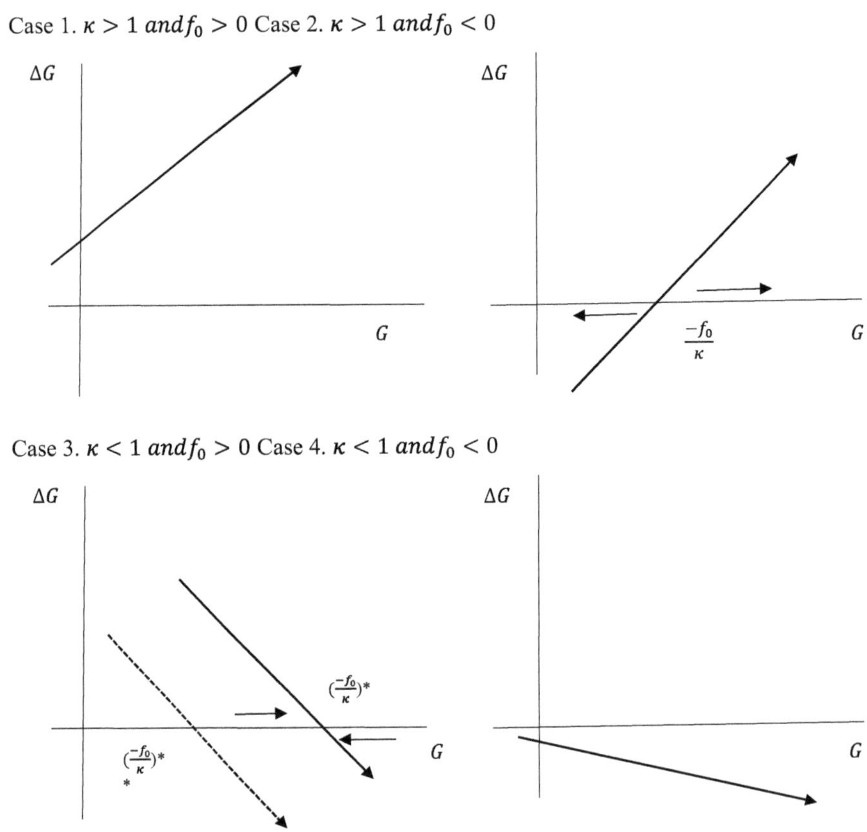

Figure 2.11 Potential scenarios

$(1 - \beta_h)$ is likely to be high, and the asset income earned by children of the elite class (μ_h) is likely to exceed that of children from the ordinary citizen class. Naturally, if the political power of elite parents is also superior, the government's education subsidies are concentrated on the children of the elite class, which further widens the income gap between the elite class and the ordinary citizen class in the child generation. In Case 1, the income gap in the child generation increases relative to the gap in the parent generation regardless of the income gap in the parent generation.

Case 2 represents a different dynamic around $\frac{-f_0}{\kappa}$. If the income gap in the parent generation is sufficiently large $\left(G_t > \frac{-f_0}{\kappa}\right)$, the gap in the child generation is wider than in the parent generation, exacerbating income inequality. Conversely, if the income gap in the parent generation is below a certain level $\left(G_t < \frac{-f_0}{\kappa}\right)$, the income gap in the child generation decreases relative to the income gap in the parent generation. In Case 2, the return on investment in human capital accumulated through education is as high as in Case 1 $(\kappa > 1)$. With a sufficiently high return on educational investment, a large enough income gap in the parent generation $\left(G_t > \frac{-f_0}{\kappa}\right)$ leads to a disparity in educational spending by parents, which results in worsening income inequality in the child generation. In this case, the income gap in the child generation increases despite government efforts to redistribute income. On the other hand, if the income gap in the parent generation is small enough $\left(G_t < \frac{-f_0}{\kappa}\right)$, the disparity in educational spending by parents decreases. And if the human capital accumulated through on-the-job training of ordinary citizen-class children $(\bar{e}_l)$ is sufficiently high, or if education subsidies are focused on the children of the ordinary-citizen class, the income gap between the elite and ordinary-citizen classes decreases in the child generation.

In Case 3, the return on investment in human capital accumulated through education is relatively low $(\kappa < 1)$. However, if the education subsidies are primarily directed to elite-class children, or if the asset income of the elite-class children is high, then the income gap in the child generation converges on the equilibrium income gap of the parent generation $\left(\frac{-f_0}{\kappa}\right)$. Therefore, the income gap between the parent and child generations does not improve from one generation to the next. Of course, if the political power of the ordinary-citizen class is so strong that the subsidies for education are concentrated on the ordinary-citizen class, or if the accumulation of human capital through on-the-job training of the ordinary-citizen class is strong, the equilibrium income gap shifts from $\left(\frac{-f_0}{\kappa}\right)^*$ to $\left(\frac{-f_0}{\kappa}\right)^{**}$.

In Case 4, the return on investment in human capital is low $(\kappa < 1)$. If the political power of the ordinary-citizen class is so strong that education subsidies are concentrated on the children of the ordinary-citizen class, or if the accumulation of human capital from on-the-job training of the ordinary-citizen class is high, then the income gap between the elite class and the ordinary-citizen class decreases in the child generation regardless of the income gap in the parent generation. This pertains to the situation in Northern Europe.[7]

2.3.4 Equalizing effects of democracy

M-R argued for the equalizing effects of democracy, asserting that if income inequality increases under democracy, the majority of citizens will support income redistribution policies, which will eventually reduce income inequality levels. However, despite the increase in income inequality since the 1980s, very few civic groups have used their political influence to advocate for higher taxes on the wealthy, and income has not been effectively redistributed. Instead, a small number of the wealthy have used their economic positions to disproportionately influence political decision-making, effecting changes to policies and systems that favor themselves, thereby monopolizing market opportunities (Stiglitz, 2012). In other words, the equalizing effects of democracy have not functioned as M-R claimed.

Using the above model, we explain why the M-R hypothesis has not materialized in the real world.

i) M-R's Case: $\gamma = 1$ and $n_h = n_l = 1$
M-R assume a pure democracy where decisions are made through majority rule; thus, the M-R case describes conditions of $\gamma = 1$ in equation 2.23 and and $n_h = n_l = 1$ in equation 2.13. In this scenario, complete democratization has been achieved ($\gamma = 1$) and members of each class vote in the interests of their own class ($n_h = n_l = 1$). In equation 2.23, the political powers of the elite and ordinary-citizen classes are proportional only to their respective populations, so political decisions are made and income is redistributed in accordance with the wishes of the ordinary-citizen class, which constitutes the majority of the population.

$$PO_{h,t} - PO_{l,t} = \log\frac{\varnothing}{1-\varnothing} < 0 \qquad (2.23)$$

In this case, education subsidies (or income redistribution) are passed on to the ordinary-citizen class, and $f_0 < 0$ if δ_l is large enough. As a result, the income gap is reduced in the child generation. In Cases 2 and 4 in Figure 2.11, income inequality in the child generation is reduced.

However, the M-R hypothesis fails to materialize under conditions of low ordinary-citizen class voter turnout ($0 < n_l < 1$) and under a captured democracy.

ii) Captured democracy: $0 < \gamma < 1$ and $n_h = n_l = 1$

$$PO_{h,t} - PO_{l,t} = \log\left(\frac{\varnothing}{(1-\varnothing)}\right)^{\gamma}\left(\frac{\varnothing\beta_h\Upsilon_{h,t}}{(1-\varnothing)\beta_l\Upsilon_{l,t}}\right)^{1-\gamma} > 0 \tag{2.24}$$

If the elite class invests heavily in *de facto* political power in equation 2.24, the political power of the elite class surpasses that of the ordinary-citizen class. If this occurs, education subsidies are directed to elite class children, and $f_0 > 0$ if δ_h is large enough. In this case, the income gap in the child generation is widened relative to the parent generation (Case 1 of Figure 2.11), or the income gap in the parent generation is maintained without reducing the income gap in the child generation (Case 3 of Figure 2.11). Thus, if the elite class, which is a numerical minority, fully invests in *de facto* political power, and the political power of the elite class comes to dominate the political system, then income is redistributed from the ordinary-citizen class to the elite class. As a result, inequality in the child generation expands or remains the same relative to inequality in the parent generation.

iii) Ordinary citizens fail to exploit their numerical advantages due to the following reasons: $\gamma = 1$ and $n_h \varnothing > n_l(1 - \varnothing)$

$$P_{h,t} - P_{l,t} = \log\frac{n_h\varnothing}{n_l(1-\varnothing)} > 0 \tag{2.25}$$

Among ordinary citizens, high illiteracy, opportunistic behavior, and government corruption result in low voter turnout or distrust of government-led income redistribution policies. In this scenario, the number of actual voters in the elite class may surpass that of actual voters from the ordinary-citizen class, so that the political power of the elite class dominates. In this case, education subsidies are directed toward the children of the elite class. As in the case of a captured democracy, inequality in the child generation expands or remains the same relative to inequality in the parent generation.

In a captured democracy or when ordinary citizens fail to exploit their numerical advantage, income is not adequately redistributed, an outcome that contravenes expectations under the M-R model.

2.4 Summary

This chapter examines how income inequality, inequality of opportunity, and political inequality are interrelated by building a model comprising two classes—the elite class and the ordinary-citizen class. We introduce a function for the determination of political power wherein the political power of each class is determined not only by population, but also by *de facto* political power, which is influenced by income. This political power further influences the adoption of policies, which in turn affect inequality of opportunity and income inequality.

We also examine how income inequality promotes inequality of opportunity by considering an intergenerational income transmission equation mediated by human capital accumulation and consider whether inequality of opportunity increases income inequality from generation to generation. Our research emphasizes that income inequality is not limited to a single generation, but is passed on, and that the accumulation of human capital of children is influenced by parental background and wealth. We also consider how political inequality affects inequality of opportunity and income inequality by finding that political power determines the allocation of education subsidies, which further influences the accumulation of human capital.

Therefore, this chapter describes the contemporaneous increase in various types of inequality rising on a global level by investigating the cumulative causal relationships among these types of inequality.

Using this model, we find that, contrary to the assertion by M-R, when political inequality and inequality of opportunity rise, democracies may struggle to solve the problem of income inequality through the voting process. Contrary to the prediction made by M-R, the equalizing effects of democracy do not function as expected in a captured democracy in which income inequality in the economic domain creates political inequality in the political domain, or when there are cleavages in the ordinary-citizen class or the voter turnout rate of the ordinary-citizen class falls for various reasons.

The cumulative increases in the types of inequality described in this chapter suggest that issues of income inequality are not limited to the economic realm, and that income inequality also affects other areas of society, including politics. This study further confirms the need for political reform—as well as improvements in other areas of society—to mitigate income inequality (Boyer, 2015).

Appendix 1

Measuring inequality of opportunity

Measuring the degree of equality of opportunity in a society involves assessing the extent to which observed inequality can be attributed to individual responsibility. One approach is to gauge the proportion of inequality in outcomes that results from factors within an individual's control. Essentially, this method seeks to determine the fairness of a society by examining the distribution of responsibility for the observed disparities. For instance, if a significant portion of income inequality among individuals is linked to environmental factors beyond their control, it suggests a lack of equal opportunities in that society.

In such a case, the realization of distributive justice may be deemed inadequate. On the other hand, if individual effort is a primary driver of inequality, the society may be considered more equitable in terms of opportunities. In summary, the measurement of equality of opportunity involves dissecting the sources of inequality, distinguishing between factors influenced by the individual and those dictated by the environment. This analysis helps evaluate whether a society is achieving a fair distribution of opportunities and promoting justice in its social and economic structures.

Since the 1990s, economists have actively embraced arguments put forth by political philosophers, employing various methods to analyze socio-economic inequality with a focus on the interplay between individual effort and performance. Notable attempts to delve into this area include works by Roemer (1998), Fleurbaey (1994), and Bossert (1995). Following Roemer's pioneering efforts in 1998, diverse methodologies were introduced to measure the degree of inequality of opportunity. Empirical studies have also surfaced, examining the extent to which economic policies, such as tax policies, have contributed to ameliorating opportunity inequality (Roemer et al., 2003). Roemer provided clarity to the concept of equality of opportunity, asserting that personal achievements, encompassing income, wealth, health, etc., are influenced by factors within an individual's control (termed effort) and those beyond an individual's control (referred to as circumstances). An example of the former is an individual's education and human capital, representing an investment that can be controlled. Circumstances, on the other hand, involve variables like gender, race, family background, or place of birth, which individuals cannot choose.

Achieving equality of opportunity, according to Roemer, involves eliminating disparities arising from differences in circumstances and increasing effort between individuals with the same circumstances. It signifies recognizing variations in economic achievement due to discrepancies in effort. In essence, the pursuit of equality of opportunity seeks to level the playing field by addressing environmental disparities and fostering a more equitable distribution of effort among individuals. Existing studies that dissect inequality of achievement into two components—inequality of opportunity (related to the environment) and inequality of effort—tend to fall into two broad categories: parametric and non-parametric methods. Parametric methods involve estimating coefficients through regression analysis between an individual's income and various influencing variables. This estimation is then used to calculate a hypothetical income achieved solely through effort. In other words, it calculates an income that would exist if environmental factors were the same for all individuals. Subsequently, the inequality index of actual income and the inequality index of this hypothetical income are computed using metrics like the Gini coefficient or entropy index. The disparity between these two indices is interpreted as the extent of opportunity inequality. On the other hand, non-parametric methods categorize the sample group into types and segments based on factors such as gender, race, education level, and level of effort. These groups are then analyzed for between-group and within-group inequality components. This approach aims to understand the differences in achievement between various categories and the variations within each category. In summary, parametric methods utilize regression analysis to estimate hypothetical incomes based on effort, while non-parametric methods categorize the sample into groups to assess both between-group and within-group inequalities. Both approaches contribute to our understanding of the multifaceted nature of inequality of opportunity and effort in society.

Numerous overseas studies have employed the described methodology to estimate the level of opportunity inequality in various countries. Bourguignon et al. (2007) and Ferreira and Gignoux (2011) are noteworthy examples of studies utilizing parametric methods, while Checchi and Peragine (2010) represent studies employing non-parametric methods. Moreover, Barros et al. (2009) and Brunori et al. (2013) have conducted comprehensive comparative studies on opportunity inequality, encompassing 41 countries globally and 7 countries in South America, using parametric and non-parametric methods, respectively.

In these studies, empirical analyses incorporated environmental factors influencing opportunity inequality, such as parents' educational background or occupation, as well as individual characteristics like gender and place of birth. The findings revealed that a portion of actual income inequality is attributable to environmental factors—termed opportunity—rather than an individual's own efforts. This suggests that some inequality in outcomes is rooted in disparities in opportunity, highlighting the significance of addressing these environmental factors to achieve a more equitable distribution of opportunities and outcomes in societies worldwide.

Roemer's method of decomposing inequality of opportunity

Roemer's method of decomposing inequality of opportunity involves breaking down overall income inequality into two distinct components: one attributed to circumstances beyond an individual's control (environmental factors) and the other attributed to individual effort. This decomposition helps to quantify the extent to which observed income disparities are a result of factors individuals can control versus those they cannot.

Let's consider the assumption proposed by Roemer where individual i's income is determined by two main factors: the environment and individual i's efforts. Notably, it's emphasized that the individual has no control over the environmental factors influencing their income. This assumption provides a conceptual framework for understanding the sources of income inequality and lays the foundation for discussions on equality of opportunity.

$$w_i = f\left(C_i, E_i, u_i\right) \tag{A1.1}$$

Here, w represents the individual's income, C is the environment, E is effort, and u represents other unobserved factors. Importantly, it is acknowledged that an individual's efforts can be shaped by the environment. Given this relationship, we can posit the following equation (A1.2).

$$w_i = f\left(C_i, E_i\left(C_i, v_i\right), u_i\right) \tag{A1.2}$$

where v represents additional factors influencing effort.

To quantify the level of inequality of opportunity, the initial step involves estimating an individual's hypothetical income under the assumption that all individuals share an equal environment. Referring to equation (A1.3), there are two distinct pathways through which the environment influences income. In both scenarios, we can derive the hypothetical income ($\tilde{w}$) when the environment is standardized to $\bar{C}$.

$$\widetilde{w_i} = \mathrm{f}\left(\bar{C}, E\left(\bar{C}, v_i\right), u_i\right) \tag{A1.3}$$

Based on equation (A1.3), the inequality level $\mathrm{I}\left(\tilde{\varnothing}\right)$ of an individual's virtual income $\tilde{w}$ can be obtained using the inequality index. This refers to the level of income inequality caused only by differences in the effort that individuals can choose.

By utilizing this index along with equation (A1.4), it is feasible to decompose the contribution of opportunity inequality to the overall income inequality.

$$\theta_I = \frac{I(\varnothing) - I\left(\tilde{\varnothing}\right)}{I(\varnothing)} \tag{A1.4}$$

Here, θ_I signifies the degree of contribution of opportunity inequality to overall income inequality, encompassing both the direct impact of the environment on income and the indirect effect of the environment influencing income through effort. Both $\varnothing$ and $\tilde{\varnothing}$ denote income distributions. $I(\varnothing) - I(\tilde{\varnothing})$, calculated as the difference between actual income inequality and the level of inequality derived under hypothetical income, serves as a measure of the extent of opportunity inequality arising from disparities in the environment. In essence, $I(\varnothing) - I(\tilde{\varnothing})$ captures the comprehensive influence of environment.

Examining equation (A1.2), it becomes evident that individual i's income is expressed as a function of the environment. Consequently, in order to analyze the contribution of opportunity inequality to income inequality, the abbreviated form of equation (A1.5) is estimated.

$$\ln\left(w_i\right) = C_i\varphi + \epsilon_i \tag{A1.5}$$

And if the estimation result of this abbreviated equation is satisfactory, the following equation (A1.6) is estimated using the estimation coefficient $\hat{\varphi}$.

$$\widetilde{w_i} = \exp\left(\bar{C}\hat{\varphi} + \hat{\epsilon_i}\right) \quad \text{(A1.6)}$$

The estimated value for equation (A1.6) corresponds to the hypothetical income from equation (A1.2), assuming a uniform environment. By applying equation (A1.6), we can observe equation (A1.4).

equation (A1.7) serves to control solely the 'direct effect' of the environment on income in equation (A1.2). It represents the hypothetical income assuming that the environment is the same in the direct effect path.

$$w_i^d = f\left(\bar{C}, E\left(C_i, v_i\right), u_i\right) \quad \text{(A1.7)}$$

Upon deriving estimates from equation (A1.7), the direct influence of the environment on income, denoting the contribution of the direct effect, can be computed using equation (A1.8) in the subsequent steps:

$$\theta_i^d = \frac{I(\varnothing) - I\left(\phi^d\right)}{I(\varnothing)} \quad \text{(A1.8)}$$

And the degree of contribution of the environment's impact on income through effort, known as the indirect effect, can be computed in the following manner:

$$\theta_I^i = \theta_I - \theta_I^d \quad \text{(A1.9)}$$

To separately estimate direct effects and indirect effects, it is necessary to estimate an extended equation that incorporates individual efforts, as outlined below:

$$\ln\left(w_i\right) = C_i\alpha + E_i\beta + u_i \quad \text{(A1.10)}$$

If the estimation result of equation (A1.10) is satisfactory, the hypothetical income as in equation (A1.11) is estimated using the estimates $\hat{\alpha}$ and $\hat{\beta}$ of α and β.

$$w_i^d = \exp\left(\bar{C}\hat{\alpha} + E_i\hat{\beta} + \hat{u_i}\right) \quad \text{(A1.11)}$$

Upon estimating equation (A1.11), it becomes possible to observe the contribution of the direct effect to income inequality using the results obtained from equation (A1.8).

Appendix 2

The role of welfare systems and trade unions in reducing inequality: The case of the Nordic countries

Throughout this chapter, we have witnessed a simultaneous increase in three forms of inequality—income inequality, political inequality, and inequality of opportunity—in numerous countries across the globe. Additionally, we delved into the interplay between these inequalities, analyzing their logical progression and outcomes using our model. Remarkably, it was confirmed that reducing income inequality in the younger generation, compared to their parents' generation, is feasible when the college wage premium is low, and the actual political power of the citizen class outweighs that of the elite. Now, the pressing question is: What practical policy options exist to mitigate the surge in these various inequalities? Various policy alternatives have been proposed to tackle income polarization and the escalating inequality, which has intensified since the global financial crisis. These proposals encompass tax reform, increasing the minimum wage, fostering equal educational opportunities, and bolstering the social safety net. Rather than conducting a systematic examination of these alternatives, our objective is to uncover clues that address the cumulative increase in various inequalities by exploring the roles of welfare systems and labor unions in resolving political inequality and inequality of opportunity.

The research findings on income inequality, political inequality, and opportunity inequality clearly indicate that the Nordic countries have significantly lower levels of these three forms of inequality compared to other nations. In contrast, English-speaking countries tend to display higher degrees of inequality across various measures when compared to their counterparts (as illustrated in Table A-2.1).

When examining income inequality, measured by the after-tax Gini index, the range varies from 0.355 to 0.375 in the United Kingdom and the United States, while it falls between 0.268 to 0.286 in Northern Europe (Sweden, Finland, Norway, and Denmark). This substantial difference suggests that income inequality is notably lower in the Nordic countries.

Similarly, analyzing the degree of inequality of opportunity, represented by the elasticity of children's income against their parents' income based on the Gatsby curve, shows a range of 0.47 to 0.50 in England and the United States, compared to 0.15 to 0.27 in Northern Europe. These figures underscore the greater equality in opportunity within the Nordic region.

Examining the political inequality index, where a lower value indicates a higher degree of political inequality, the UK scores 42 and the US scores 54. In contrast, Sweden scores 89, Denmark 72, and Finland and Norway score 61 and 60, respectively. This indicates that the Nordic countries exhibit greater political equality in comparison to other developed nations. In summary, it is evident from the research that the Nordic countries show lower levels of economic, political, and opportunity inequality in comparison to the United Kingdom, the United States, and other continental European countries.

Table A-2.1 Income inequality, inequality of opportunity, and political inequality levels in major countries

	Income inequality	*Inequality of opportunity*	*Political Inequality*	*Union membership rate*	*Wage gap between high school and college graduates (High school=100)*
UK	0.355(2020)	0.50	42(2016)	23.5(2019)	146.5 (2020)
USA	0.375(2021)	0.47	54(2016)	9.9(2019)	172.8 (2020)
France	0.292(2019)	0.41	55(2016)	10.8(2016)	149.4 (2018)
Germany	0.296(2019)	0.32	60(2016)	16.3(2019)	164.5 (2020)
Sweden	0.286(2021)	0.27	89(2016)	65.2(2019)	114.8 (2020)
Finland	0.273(2021)	0.18	61 (2016)	58.8(2019)	125.6 (2019)
Norway	0.285(2021)	0.17	60(2016)	50.4(2019)	113.8 (2020)
Denmark	0.268(2019)	0.15	72 (2016)	67.0(2019)	111.1 (2020)

Note: 1) For income inequality and inequality of opportunity, the smaller the value, the more equal it is. Conversely, the higher the value of political inequality, the more equal it is; 2) Parentheses indicate the year; 3) The income inequality data is from World Inequality Database, the political inequality data is from Varieties of Democracy database, and the inequality of opportunity is derived from the elasticity of children's income against their parent's income, represented on the Y-axis in Figure 2.7. The unionization rate and wage gap between high school and college graduates were obtained from the OECD database.

While various institutional factors contribute to the inequality differences among countries, our attention is focused on the roles of welfare systems and labor unions, as depicted in Figure A-2.1 (Hacker and Pierson, 2010; Schneider and Makszin, 2014). Labor unions and welfare systems play a critical role in reducing income inequality, and they also play an essential part in addressing political inequality. As discussed earlier, political scientists (Bartel, 2008; Hacker and Pierson, 2010) attribute the rise in political inequality in the United States to the weakening of labor unions that historically represented the interests of the low-income class and the limited political participation of this group. The reasons behind their decreased political engagement are linked to factors such as restricted access to information, lower income levels, and limited opportunities to participate in social networks.

Schneider and Makszin (2014) conduct fascinating research on this topic. Their findings reveal that the lack of political participation among the low-income class is not a universal trend. In countries with robust labor union bargaining power and well-developed welfare systems, unlike the United States, individuals from the low-income and low-education groups actively engage in political activities. In countries where labor unions wield significant bargaining power and welfare systems are well-established, low-income individuals can access crucial information and knowledge essential for political participation through various educational programs provided by these institutions. Additionally, they are offered opportunities to connect with diverse social networks. Moreover, strong trade unions and well-structured welfare systems ensure higher wages and substantial social welfare benefits, which effectively address

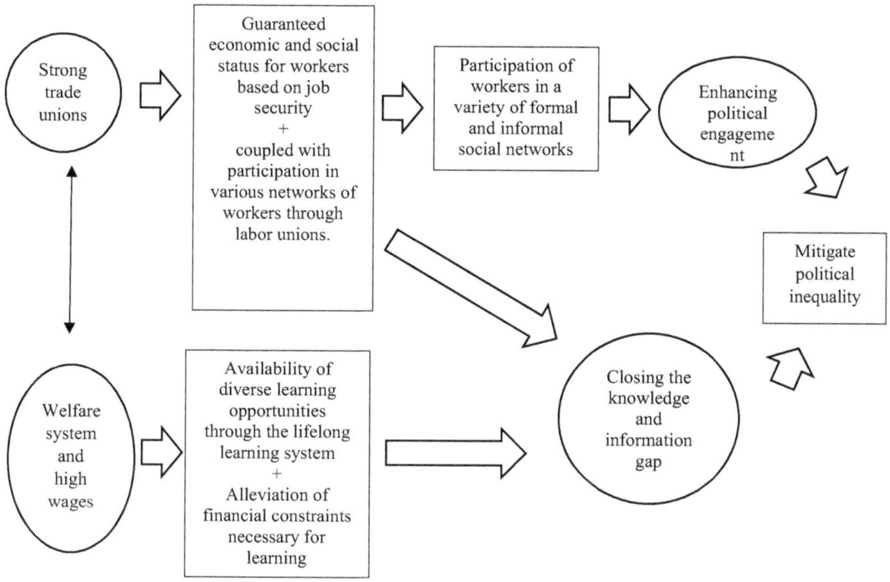

Figure A-2.1 The role of trade unions and welfare systems in mitigating political inequality

the financial barriers associated with political participation and learning. As a result, these unions and social welfare programs are believed to stimulate the political involvement of low-income groups and workers, ultimately leading to a reduction in political inequality. The researchers conduct empirical analysis on 37 countries and discover that nations with robust welfare systems and higher levels of employment protection experience smaller gaps in knowledge, information, income, and union participation rates between income groups. Their findings support the notion that well-established employment protection and welfare systems for the low-income class foster increased political engagement within this group, resulting in reduced political and income inequality.

Figure A-2.2 illustrates how Nordic countries have achieved equal income distribution, political equality, and equality of opportunity through a combination of three systems. The first system is the production or technology accumulation system. Unlike England and America, Northern Europe's production system relies on company-specific or industry-specific technology (Estebez-Abe et al., 2001), resulting in a lower educational premium. Table A-2.1 demonstrates the degree of wage premium for college graduates compared to high school graduates, with the US having the highest at 72.8%, followed by Germany at 64.5%, France at 49.4%, and the UK at 46.5%. In contrast, Northern Europe has lower levels, with Denmark having the lowest at 11.1%, followed by Norway at 13.8%, Sweden at 14.8%, and Finland at 25.6%. This lower educational premium in Northern Europe reduces the

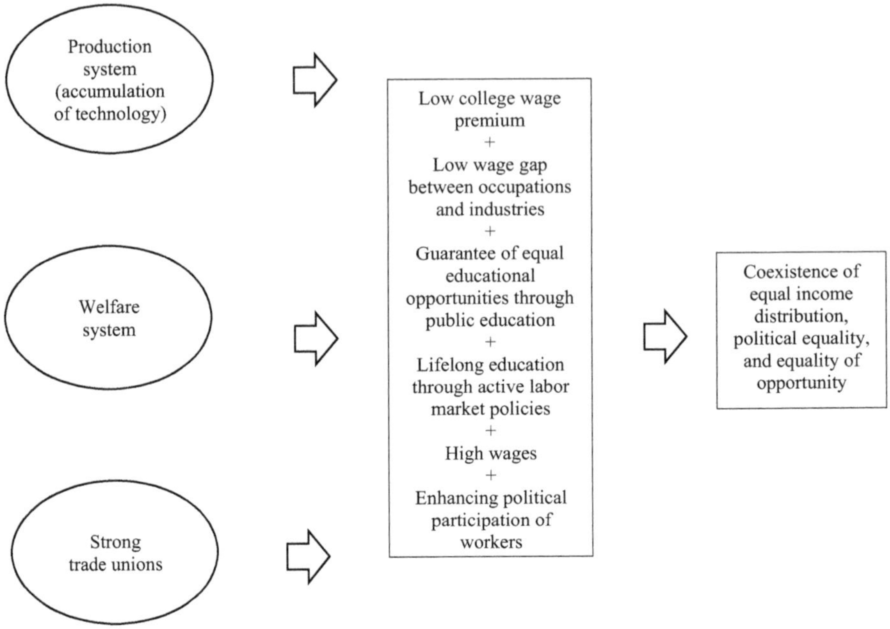

Figure A-2.2 Coexistence of equal income distribution, political equality, and equality of opportunity in Northern Europe

impact of parental income on their children's income through investment in education. Moreover, centralized collective bargaining and a solidarity wage system with equal wages for the same occupation in Northern Europe result in a smaller wage gap between industries or occupations. The well-equipped welfare system ensures equal opportunities for education through public education and lifelong learning policies as part of active labor market initiatives. This provides workers with opportunities to acquire new skills and knowledge, consequently reducing wage gaps due to skill-biased technological change and bridging the information and knowledge gap for workers' political participation. As a result, workers' political participation is promoted.

Union membership rates reflect the strength of negotiations held by trade unions. The United Kingdom and the United States have union membership rates of 23.5% and 9.9%, respectively, whereas Sweden has a rate of 65.2% and Denmark's stands at 67.0% (as indicated in Table A-2.1). Strong labor unions play a role in distributing economic performance based on bargaining power, guaranteeing high wages, and offering various programs for workers' political engagement. In this context, Miettinen (2013) reports an interesting finding that a higher proportion of people in Northern Europe participate in various social networks compared to those in continental Europe. This has become the foundation of grassroots democracy in Northern Europe, with around 90% of Danish and Swedish citizens, over 80% of Norwegians, and 76% of

Finns being members of social groups. Such groups conduct various experiments and discussions to collectively address social issues.

In conclusion, the Nordic countries achieve economic equality, political equality, and equality of opportunity concurrently through the mechanism illustrated in Figure A-2.2. On the contrary, Anglo-American countries, unlike their counterparts in Northern Europe, grapple with elevated levels of income inequality, substantial political inequality, and notable inequality of opportunity. This can be attributed to their reliance on production systems built around general-purpose technology, the presence of underdeveloped welfare systems, and lower rates of unionization.

Thomas Humphrey Marshall (1964), who elevated welfare to a universal right that should be equally enjoyed by all citizens, conducts an analysis of the historical evolution of citizenship (comprising civil, political, and social rights) with a specific focus on modern British history. He argues that although legal equality before the law exists in theory, it fails to function adequately in reality due to disparities in knowledge, information, and income among different social classes. Throughout the history of democracies, various corrective measures, such as providing legal aid, offering subsidies for legal costs to low-income individuals, and setting limits on election expenses, have been implemented by countries to address these disparities.

Additionally, Marshall posits that for the three forms of citizenship rights—civil, political, and social rights—to be sustainable, each right is interdependent on the others. This perspective finds support among scholars like Okun, Rawls, and Polanyi. Historically, social rights emerge only after civil and political rights are established, and the exercise of civil and political rights necessitates a fundamental level of social security. Without this basic security, the establishment of fair labor contracts, which form the foundation of civil rights, becomes unattainable due to wage competition at the lower end of the spectrum, and the exercise of political rights is influenced by financial power. Okun also argues for the necessity of a minimum wage system in this context, while Marshall justifies the legitimacy of social welfare systems in ensuring a civilized life.

As seen earlier, welfare systems and labor unions play a crucial role in bridging the information and knowledge gap among low-income groups and workers, thereby contributing to the realization of legal equality. Moreover, by guaranteeing a minimum standard of living for all members of society, they provide the necessary material foundation for political equality. While it is widely recognized that welfare systems and labor unions have positively contributed to reducing income inequality in the Nordic countries, they have also made significant strides in achieving political equality and equal opportunities. As a result, countries with robust welfare systems and strong labor unions, often referred to as Nordic countries, exhibit lower levels of income inequality, political inequality, and inequality of opportunity in comparison to the Anglo-American region, where the influence of welfare systems and labor unions is relatively weaker.

Since the mid-1990s, South America has achieved significant success in reducing income inequality, and this accomplishment can be attributed to the positive contributions of welfare systems and labor unions in addressing income inequality, political disparity, and unequal opportunities. While the effectiveness of these systems varies based on the capabilities of labor unions and civil society in each country, South American nations begin to recognize the importance of social welfare and income redistribution as critical political issues, especially after the Asian financial crisis in 1998, which sparks civil protests and social resistance. As a result of these developments, 11 countries in South America witness the emergence of leftist governments between 1998 and 2011, which spearhead social security system reforms (Roberts, 2012). These reforms include the institutionalization of minimum wage policies tied to price and growth rate in countries like Brazil. Moreover, they establish connections between human capital accumulation and the welfare system, along with integrating the minimum wage with various social assistance programs to ensure that diverse social classes can benefit from economic growth. These efforts lay the foundation for greater equality of opportunity by expanding educational prospects. Although this social experiment may not be deemed an unequivocal success due to challenges like insufficient investment, productivity improvement, and the impacts of globalization, it remains significant as it has altered the longstanding trend of inequality that persisted for decades.

Despite increased inequality in many countries, achieving social justice, encompassing political equality, economic equality, and equality of opportunity, is not an insurmountable goal, as demonstrated by the achievements of both Northern Europe and South America. These examples also challenge Okun's assertion of a trade-off between growth and equality. Instead, they showcase that growth and equality can complement each other through well-designed institutions, particularly robust welfare systems. Based on the lessons learned from these experiences, there is an urgent need to develop a new welfare system that fosters a virtuous cycle between social justice, welfare, and growth. Building upon these successes can lead to a more equitable and prosperous society for all.

Notes

1 We use *class* and *group* interchangeably.
2 For instance, suppose that children of the elite class attend private schools with high tuition fees, while children of the ordinary-citizen class attend public schools with little or no tuition fees. If the political power of the elite class dominates that of the ordinary-citizen class, the government's education subsidies will be concentrated on private schools. Conversely, if the political power of the ordinary-citizen class is superior to that of the elite class, the education subsidies will be concentrated on public schools.
3 Acemoglu and Robinson (2006) define political power as a group's ability to pursue and develop its preferred policies despite the resistance of other groups.
4 In the United States, the low-income voter turnout rate is less than 50% due to economic struggles and high illiteracy rates. Conversely, voter participation among

the wealthy is around 90%. Additionally, 56% of the wealthy made political donations, while only 6% of low-income families did so. In fact, the top 0.01% accounted for 40% of total political donations. Three-quarters of the wealthy were involved in political activities. This contrasts with only 13% of the poor (American Political Science Association Task Force, 2004; Bonica et al., 2013).

5 Class-betrayal voting refers to lower-income voters or higher-income voters voting for higher-income class or lower-income class interests, respectively. Our model, however, excludes class-betrayal voting. We posit that lower-income voters who do not support lower-income class issues simply abstain from voting.

6 Given that the population of each class is assumed to be fixed and the income of each class member is assumed to be the same, the degree of income inequality between classes $\left(\frac{\phi Y_{h,t}}{(1-\phi)Y_{l,t}}\right)$ is proportional to the income gap between representative parents $\left(\frac{Y_{h,t}}{Y_{l,t}}\right)$.

7 Details regarding the Nordic experience can be found in Appendix 2.

References

Acemoglu, D., S. Restrepo, and J. Robinson (2013), "Democracy, redistribution and inequality," *NBER Working Paper*, No. 19746.

Acemoglu, D. and J. Robinson (2008), "Persistence of power, elites, and institutions," *American Economic Review*, Vol. 98, No. 1, pp. 267–293.

Acemoglu, D. and J. Robinson (2006), *Economic Origins of Dictatorship and Democracy*, New York: Cambridge University Press.

American Political Science Association Task Force (2004), "American democracy in an age of rising inequality," *Perspectives on Politics*, Vol. 2, No. 4, pp. 651–666.

Bailey, M. J. and S. M. Dynarski (2011), "Inequality in postsecondary education," In Greg J. Duncan and Richard J. Murnane (eds), *Whither opportunity? Rising inequality, schools, and children's life chances*, New York: Russell Sage Foundation.

Bartel, L. (2008), *Unequal democracy: The political economy of a new gilded age*, Princeton, NJ: Princeton University Press.

Barros, R., F.H.G. Ferreira, J.R. Molinas, and J. Saavedra (2009), *Measuring inequality of opportunities in Latin America and the Caribbean*, Washington, DC: World Bank Publications.

Bonica, A., N. McCarty, K. Poole, and H. Rosenthal (2013), "Why hasn't democracy slowed rising inequality?" *Journal of Economic Perspectives*, Vol. 27, No. 3, pp. 103–124.

Bossert, W. (1995), "Redistribution mechanisms based on individual characteristics," *Mathematical Social Sciences*, Vol. 29, No. 1, pp. 1–17.

Bourguignon, F., F.H. Ferreira, and M. Menendez (2007), "Inequality of opportunity in Brazil," *Review of income and Wealth*, Vol. 53, No. 4, pp. 585–618.

Boyer, R. (2015), *Économie politique des capitalisms*, Paris: La Découverte.

Brunori, P., F. H. Ferreira, and V. Peragine (2013), "Inequality of opportunity, income inequality and economic mobility: some international comparisons," *World Bank Policy Research Working Paper*, 6304.

Checchi, D. and V. Peragine (2010), "Inequality of opportunity in Italy," *The Journal of Economic Inequality*, Vol. 8, No. 4, pp. 429–450.

Choi, G. (2021), "Conceptualizing and measuring political inequality in a cross-national perspective," *Comparative Sociology*, Vol. 20, No. 1, pp. 1–44.

Cole, W.M. (2018), "Poor and powerless: Economic and political inequality in cross-national perspective, 1981–2011," *International Sociology*, Vol. 33, No. 3, pp. 357–385.

Corak, M. (2013), "Income inequality, equality of opportunity, and intergenerational mobility," *Journal of Economic Perspectives*, Vol. 27, No. 3, pp. 79–102.

Dubrow, J. (2010), "Cross-national measures of political inequality of voice," *ASK*, Vol. 19, No. 1, pp. 93–110.
Estevez-Abe, M., T. Iversen and D. Soskice (2001), "Social protection and the formation of skills: a reinterpretation of the welfare state," In A. Hall and D. Soskice (eds), *Varieties of capitalism: The institutional foundations of comparative advantage*, Oxford: Oxford University Press.
Ferreira, F.H. and J. Gignoux (2011), "The measurement of inequality of opportunity: Theory and an application to Latin America," *Review of Income and Wealth*, Vol. 57, No. 4, pp. 622–657.
Ferreira, F. and V. Peragine (2015), "Equality of opportunity: Theory and evidence," *Policy Research Working Paper*, No. 7217, World Bank.
Fleurbaey, M. (1994), "On fair compensation," *Theory and Decision*, Vol. 36, No. 3, pp. 277–307.
Hacker, J. and P. Pierson (2010), *Winner-take-all politics: How Washington made the rich richer and turned its back on the middle class*, New York: Simon & Schuster Paperbacks.
Houle, C. (2018), "Does economic inequality breed political inequality?," *Democratization*, Vol. 25, No. 8, pp. 1500–1518.
ILO (2011), *G 20 country policy briefs*, Geneva: ILO.
Levy, S. and N. Schady (2013), "Latin America's policy change: Education, social insurance, redistribution," *Journal of Economic Perspectives*, Vol. 27, No. 2, pp. 193–218.
Lustig, N., L. Lopez-Calva and E. Ortiz-Juarez (2013), "Declining inequality in Latin America in the 2000s: The cases of Argentina, Brazil, and Mexico," *Development*, Vol. 44, pp. 129–141.
Marshall, T. H. (1964), *Class, citizenship, and social development*, Garden City: Doubleday and Company.
Meltzer, A. H. and S. F. Richard (1981), "A rational theory of the size of government," *Journal of Political Economy*, Vol. 89, No. 5, pp. 914–927.
Miettinen, R. (2013), *Innovation, human capabilities, and democracy*, Oxford: Oxford University Press.
OECD (2011), *Divided we stand: Why inequality keeps rising*, Paris: OECD.
Piketty, T. (2014), *Capital in the twenty-first century*, Cambridge, MA: The Belknap Press of Harvard University Press.
Piketty, T. and E. Saez, (2007), "How progressive is the U.S. federal tax system? A historical and international perspective," *Journal of Economic Perspectives*, Vol. 21, No. 1, pp. 3–24.
Przeworski, A. (2014), "Choices and echoes: Stability and change of policy regimes," in Magara, E. (ed), *Economic crises and policy regimes*, pp 33–55, Cheltenham: Edward Elgar Publishing Limited.
Rawls, J. (1999), *A theory of justice*, Revised Edition, Cambridge, MA: Harvard University Press.
Roberts, K. M. (2012), "The politics of inequality and redistribution in Latin America's post-adjustment era," *UN-WIDER Working Paper*, No. 2012/08.
Roemer, J.E. (1998), Equality of opportunity, Cambridge, MA: Harvard University Press.
Roemer, J.E., R. Aaberge, U. Colombino, J. Fritzell, S. P. Jenkins, I. Marx, M. Page, E. Pommer, J. Ruiz-Castillo, M.J.S. Segundo, T. Traanes, G. Wagner, and I. Zubiri (2003), "To what extent do fiscal regimes equalize opportunities for income acquisition among citizens?" *Journal of Public Economics*, Vol. 87, No. 3–4, pp. 539–565.
Rothstein, B. (2005), *Social traps and the problem of trust*, Cambridge: Cambridge University Press.
Schattschneider, E. E. (1960), *The semi-sovereign people: A realist view of democracy in America*, New York: Holt, Rinehart and Winston

Schneider, C. and K. Makszin (2014), “Forms of welfare capitalism and education-based participatory inequality”, *Socio-Economic Review*, Vol. 12, No. 2, pp. 437–462.
Solon, G. (2004), “A model of intergenerational mobility variation over time and place,” In M. Corak (ed), *Generational income mobility in North America and Europe*, Cambridge: Cambridge University Press.
Stiglitz, J. E. (2012), *The price of inequality: How today's divided society endangers our future*, New York: W.W. Norton & Company.
World Inequality Lab (2017), *World Inequality Report 2018*, http://wir2018.wid.world/

Database

OECD database (https://data.oecd.org/, retrieved on August 24, 2023).
Varieties of Democracy database (https://v-dem.net/data/the-v-dem-dataset/, retrieved on August 24, 2023).
World Inequality Database (https://wid.world/, retrieved on August 24, 2023).

3 Can democracy effectively mitigate the simultaneous rise of different forms of inequality?

Democracy's evolution has been influenced by various cleavages and conflicts, such as the separation of church and state, the conflict between capital and labor, the divide between urban and rural areas, and the distinction between the periphery and the center. The intersection of these cleavages has significantly shaped the diverse party systems observed in different countries. Schattschneider (1960) underscores that in contemporary socio-political contexts, a critical cleavage comparable to historical experiences in the West is the divide between business and government, or between economic power and political power. The relationship between these two entities plays a pivotal role in shaping the structure of contemporary societies. Berle and Means (1932), considered pioneers in corporate governance theory, posited that the emergence of large modern corporations led to the concentration of economic power. This concentration, in turn, enabled these corporations to compete with the government on an equal footing, ultimately positioning them to potentially surpass the government in the future. They projected that modern corporations, wielding power comparable to premodern churches, would become akin to governments in terms of resource mobilization and organizational size. Thus, it is not an exaggeration to state that the relationship between business and government, or between economic power and political power, defines the character of each country's political system and society.

Schattschneider (1960) contended that democracy, fundamentally, is an alternative power structure that offers institutions and policy instruments to counterbalance the inequalities generated by economic power. Through this, citizens' political and economic interests are safeguarded from economic power. In the field of economics, building on earlier studies by Downs (1957) and Romer (1975), M-R (Meltzer and Richard, 1981) also propose that democracy can serve as a mechanism that promotes income redistribution through the implementation of institutions and policies, thereby mitigating income inequality and protecting the economic interests of low-income and impoverished groups. In a democracy, the majority's enfranchisement often results in heightened public support for income redistribution policies, potentially mitigating income inequality. Economists hold an optimistic view that

DOI: 10.4324/9781032695754-3

democracy, consistent with M-R predictions, can effectively address these inequalities, even amidst the concurrent rise of multiple inequalities.

Both Schattschneider, a political scientist, and M-R, a pair of economists, recognized the threat of income inequality stemming from economic power in a market economy, endorsing democracy as a potential remedy. In a democratic system where citizens are granted voting rights, individuals foster hopeful beliefs that various forms of inequality can be tackled through policy formulation, institutional arrangements, and resource redistribution.

M-R, drawing from Tocqueville's ideas, underscores that the extent of income redistribution by the government depends on two factors: the breadth of suffrage and the level of pre-tax income inequality. The hypothesis posits that the interaction between the economic domain (pre-tax income inequality) and the political domain (the extent of suffrage) determines the degree of income redistribution within a society. By broadening suffrage to encompass a wider population, regardless of their income levels, and establishing a political system that advocates for the interests of lower-income groups, M-R argues that income inequality can be mitigated through redistribution, even if it intensifies in the economic domain. M-R also identifies the individuals who hold the power to influence income redistribution in a society as *decisive voters*, and their identity is shaped by the nature of the political system. In a dictatorship, this role is assumed by the dictator, while in a democratic majority rule, it is the median voter. As suffrage expands to include more lower-income groups, the income level of the median voter decreases, leading to an increased demand for redistribution. Building on this, M-R believed that democracy had the potential to alleviate diverse inequalities brought about by the market economy, and economists maintained an optimistic view regarding the varied inequalities that could emerge, as predicted by M-R.

3.1 Explaining the M-R hypothesis through modeling

In this section, we aim to model a comparison of income redistribution disparities between two contrasting scenarios: autocracy and democracy. Our goal is to elucidate how the equalizing effects, as assumed by M-R, function within a democratic context. Furthermore, Chapter 4 extends the model formulated in this chapter to explain the disparity between the expected and actual outcomes of democracy's equalization effect, which is the focal point of our discussion.

3.1.1 Basic assumptions

We assume that a country is divided into three groups based on income level: l represents the lower-income class, m the middle-income class, and h the higher-income class. Total income (M) and total population (N) are fixed and standardized at 1. The shares of lower-, middle- and higher-income class income to total income are represented by a_h,a_m, and a_l, respectively. These shares represent the before-taxes-and-transfers income (or market income) of each class.

$$a_h + a_m + a_l = 1 \tag{3.1}$$

We assume that $a_h > \frac{1}{2}$, $a_m > 0$ and $a_l > 0$

The level of market-income inequality is measured by the gap between the income share of the higher-income class (a_h) and that of other classes ($1 - a_h$). Thus, $a_h - \frac{1}{2}$ represents the level of market-income inequality and the degree of class cleavage (Rodrik and Mukand, 2016).

The shares of the population for the lower-, middle- and higher-income classes are denoted by n_h, n_m, and n_l, respectively. These three variables total a value of 1, and it is assumed that the total population and the population share of each class are fixed.

$$n_h + n_m + n_l = 1 \tag{3.2}$$

Furthermore, the middle-class population share is assumed to be larger than the lower- and higher-income classes: $n_m > n_l$ and $n_m > n_h$.

The utility of class i (u_i) in Equation 3.3 depends on the respective class's post-taxes-and-transfers income (or disposable income) (y_i), which is determined by Equation 3.4.

$$u_i = y_i \tag{3.3}$$

$$y_i = (1 - t)a_i + \widehat{g_i} \tag{3.4}$$

$$\widehat{g_i} = g_i - n_i c \frac{g^2}{2} - \gamma_i \left(g_i - n_i c \frac{g^2}{2} \right) > 0 \tag{3.5}$$

$$= (1 - \gamma_i) \left(g_i - n_i c \frac{g^2}{2} \right)$$

where $i \in \{h, m, l\}$, $t > 0$, $c > 0$, $0 \leq \gamma_i < 1$, $\widehat{g_i} > 0$, and $g = g_h + g_m + g_l = t$.

t in Equation 3.4 signifies the tax rate, which is equally applied to all three classes. $\widehat{g_i}$ represents the net in-kind transfers provided by the government, which are redistributed to class i in the form of in-kind transfers. The government collects taxes from each class and distributes in-kind transfers, but some loss (or leakage) occurs during the processes of tax collection and redistribution. Equation 3.5 defines net in-kind transfers ($\widehat{g_i}$), which are solely redistributed to class i. g_i denotes the gross redistribution received by class i in the absence of leakage in the redistribution process. Two distinct reasons account for these losses: *Okun-type leakage* and *Waldfogel-type loss*.

In the *leaky bucket theory*, Okun (1975) posited that the government would lose resources during the process of tax collection and income transfer. He highlighted that the maintenance costs (e.g., purchasing computers, employing staff, legal services, documentation) incurred during the tax transfer process are a typical source of leakage. Based on Okun's theory, we assume that leakage will increase quadratically as the total amount of government redistribution (g) increases $\left(c\frac{g^2}{2}\right)$. Here, c represents the parameter of the first type of loss incurred during collection and transfer. The loss borne by each class depends on the population share of each class (n_i): $n_i c\frac{g^2}{2}$.

The second type of loss, akin to Waldfogel's (2001) deadweight loss of Christmas gifts, arises from the mismatch between the type of in-kind transfer preferred by each class and the type actually provided. This loss occurs because the government collectively transfers income, rather than tailoring income transfers to the preferences of each class. Parameter γ_i represents this second type of loss. If class i receives its preferred type of transfer, γ_i has a value close to zero. We assume that each class cannot consume all of the received transfers and leaves some of the unfavorable transfers $\left(\gamma_i\left(g_i - n_i c\frac{g^2}{2}\right)\right)$ unused. Therefore, of the redistributed in-kind transfers that are not lost due to the first type of leakage $\left(g_i - n_i c\frac{g^2}{2}\right)$, class i consumes only a fraction $(1 - \gamma_i)$, and γ_i represents the waste rate of in-kind transfers caused by this mismatch. Let's further assume that the type of in-kind transfer favored by each class depends on *identity*[1] (e.g., ideology or moral values).[2] Thus, if the lower- and higher-income classes share similar racial, religious, and regional identities, the types of in-kind transfers preferred by the two classes would be similar, regardless of income differences. Moreover, if a society is so homogeneous that no identity cleavages exist, then the types of in-kind transfers desired by all three classes would be identical. In this case, $\gamma_i = 0$. Therefore, two forms of cleavage exist in our model: the first being a class— or economic—cleavage, and the second being an identity cleavage, measured by γ_i.

3.1.2 The equalizing effects of democracy and the M-R model

Case 1: Autocracy

$$y_h = a_h + g - c\frac{g^2}{2} \tag{3.6}$$

$$y_m = a_m(1-t) \tag{3.7}$$

$$y_l = a_l(1-t) \tag{3.8}$$

Under autocracy, the higher-income class determines the tax rate, and the middle- and lower-income classes bear all of the tax, as depicted in Equations 3.7 and 3.8. These resources are solely used for redistribution to the higher-income class, and all losses incurred in the redistribution process are borne exclusively by the higher-income class (Equation 3.6). In this specific political regime, because only the high-income class benefits from the redistribution, and it does so without negotiating with other classes, the high-income class can decide on the form of redistribution it prefers ($\gamma_i = 0$). From this, we can derive the following equation using balanced budget constraints and Equations 3.7 and 3.8.

$$g = t\left(a_m + a_l\right) = t\left(1 - a_h\right) \tag{3.9}$$

We substitute Equation 3.9 into Equation 3.6.

$$y_h = a_h + t\left(1 - a_h\right) - \frac{ct^2\left(1 - a_h\right)^2}{2} \tag{3.10}$$

From Equation 3.10, we can then derive the tax rate (t_a) that maximizes the higher-income class's disposable income:

$$t_a = \frac{1}{c\left(1 - a_h\right)} \tag{3.11}$$

As depicted in Figure 3.1, in the higher-income class market-income interval $\left(\frac{1}{2} < a_h < 1\right)$, the higher-income class continues to raise tax rates to burden the lower- and middle-income classes, even as income inequality or economic cleavages widen, and this can be measured by $a_h - \frac{1}{2}$. The higher-income class transfers income from the middle- and lower-income classes through taxation

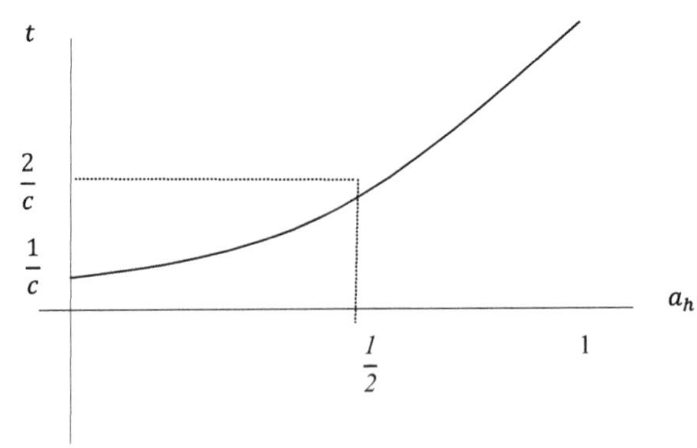

Figure 3.1 Autocracy

to increase its own earnings, making autocracy an extractive political regime (Acemoglu and Robinson, 2012).

Case 2: Democracy

Case 2 differs from case 1 in that, unlike under autocracy, the middle-income class under a democratic political system functions as the decisive voter (i.e., the median voter), with all voters (including those of the lower-income class) being granted the right to vote. Because no identity cleavages are present under this scenario, we assume $\gamma = 0$

Case 2-1: Director's law

The fact that the middle-income class forms the majority implies that $n_m > \frac{1}{2}$.

$$y_h = a_h(1-t) \tag{3.12}$$

$$y_m = a_m(1-t) + g - \frac{cg^2}{2} \tag{3.13}$$

$$y_l = a_l(1-t) \tag{3.14}$$

$$g = t(a_h + a_m + a_l) = t \tag{3.15}$$

In case 2-1, the tax rate is determined by the majority middle-income class (i.e., the decisive and median voter). In Equations 3.12, 3.13, and

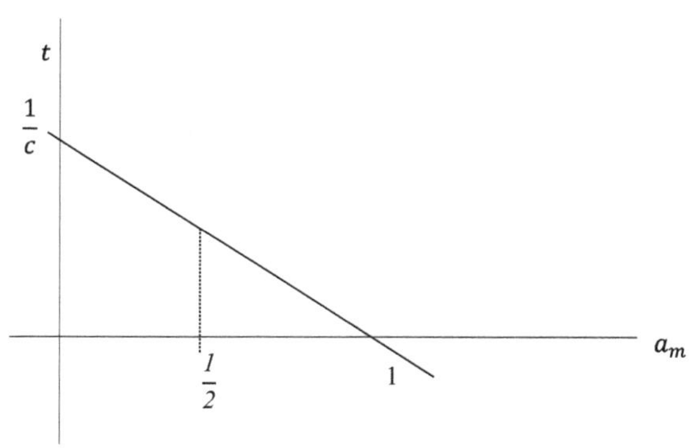

Figure 3.2 Director's law

3.14, all three classes pay taxes, while the benefits accrue to the middle-income class (Equation 3.13).

George Stigler referenced the argument of his fellow professor Director, who criticized income redistribution policy and the welfare system under such a scenario, and coined the term *Director's law* to describe this dynamic. Stigler contended that in a democracy where the majority (i.e., the middle-income class) determines tax policy, taxes are collected from the lower- and higher-income voters to benefit solely the middle-income class. In other words, democracy sacrifices the lower-income class to enrich the middle-income class.

We substitute Equation 3.15, representing the balanced budget constraint, into Equation 3.13.

$$y_m = a_m(1-t) + t - \frac{ct^2}{2} \tag{3.16}$$

The majority middle-income class then maximizes its own disposable income through a tax rate (t_{dr}) that can be derived from Equation 3.16:

$$t_{dr} = \frac{1-a_m}{c} \tag{3.17}$$

Comparing equations 3.11 and 3.17, we observe that autocracy results in a higher tax rate than under Director's law. As illustrated in Figure 3.2, since middle-class income (a_m) is between 0 and $\frac{1}{2}$, the closer a_m is to 0, the higher the tax rate applied to lower- and higher-income voters will be to distribute more tax revenue to the middle-income class. Based on Director's law, Stigler criticized such a government income redistribution policy for sacrificing the lower-income class to maximize benefits to the middle-income class.

Case 2-2:

M-R's case, $n_l < n_m < \frac{1}{2}$ and $n_m + n_l > \frac{1}{2}$, $\frac{n_m}{n_m + n_l} = n_1$ and $\frac{n_l}{n_m + n_l} = n_2$

$$y_h = a_h(1-t) \tag{3.18}$$

$$y_m = a_m(1-t) + n_1 g - \frac{cg^2}{2} n_1 \tag{3.19}$$

$$y_l = a_l(1-t) + n_2 g - \frac{cg^2}{2} n_2 \tag{3.20}$$

$$g = t\left(a_h + a_m + a_l\right) = t \tag{3.21}$$

Case 2-2 is similar to that of 2-1, with the middle-income class still being the largest of the three groups. However, under this scenario, the middle-income class cannot achieve a majority without forming a coalition with the lower-income class. We assume a political mechanism exists to coordinate the interests of the lower- and middle-income classes, and this scenario also assumes a society with a homogenous identity (thus $\gamma = 0$), such that only economic or class cleavages remain in the society because everyone holds the same identities (i.e., moral values). The middle-income class, the median voter, decides the tax rate, but taxes are paid by all three classes (Equations 3.18 to 3.20) and redistributed to both the lower- and middle-income voters. We assume that the rate of distribution is directly proportional to the lower- and middle-income class population ratios (n_1 and n_2). The result of substituting Equation 3.21, the balanced budget formula, into Equation 3.19 is shown below.

$$y_m = a_m\left(1 - t\right) + n_1 t - \frac{ct^2}{2} n_1 \tag{3.22}$$

The middle-income class, the median voter, then sets the tax rate (t_{mr}) that maximizes its disposable income, which is derived from Equation 3.22:

$$t_{mr} = \frac{n_1 - a_m}{cn_1} \tag{3.23}$$

Comparing Equations 3.17 and 3.23 reveals that the Director's law scenario results in a higher tax rate than under the M-R model.

Figure 3.3 demonstrates that the middle-income class favors higher taxation or more income redistribution as a_m falls or as the middle-income class's market income decreases.

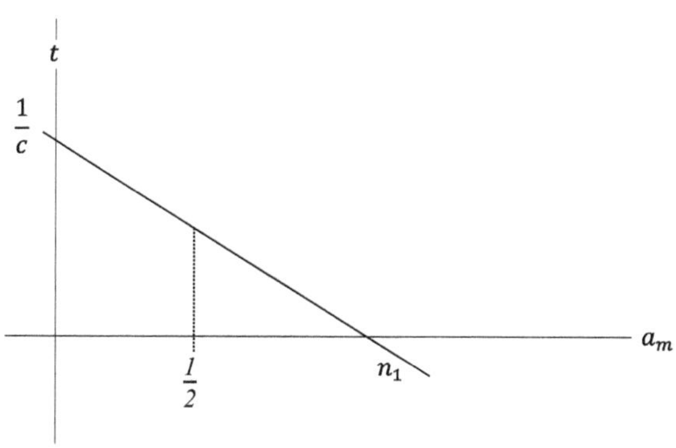

Figure 3.3 M-R model

3.2 Empirical research findings on democracy's equalizing effects

3.2.1 Significant outcomes of empirical research

In this section, we assess the validity of the M-R hypothesis by evaluating the findings from previous empirical studies related to the M-R hypothesis.

Because decisions are made on a majority basis in a democracy, as income inequality increases, the middle- and lower-income voters, who together constitute a majority, are likely to support redistribution policies. Based on this logic, M-R posited that democracy produces equalizing effects.[3] However, lower- and middle-income voters have been unable to effectively raise taxes on the wealthy even during periods of rising income inequality, and, thus, income redistribution efforts have not been successful. Rather, a small number of high earners have leveraged their economic position to influence political decisions, policy changes, and market rules to favor themselves and monopolize market opportunities (Stiglitz, 2012). In the end, the so-called equalizing effects of democracy proposed by M-R have not materialized. Empirical studies indicate that the relationships between income inequality, democracy, and redistribution are not based on a single dynamic.

Because of its significant policy and theoretical implications, the M-R hypothesis has been analyzed theoretically and empirically in various fields. However, the empirical literature on the relationship between democracy and inequality has produced ambiguous results about the validity of the M-R hypothesis (Perotti, 1996; Bassett et al., 1999; Milanovic, 2010).

These studies on the relationships between income inequality, democracy, and redistribution demonstrate that causality is not determined by single-factor dynamics. Most studies fail to clearly delineate the relationships between democracy, income inequality, and redistribution (Bollen and Grandjean, 1981; Bollen and Jackman, 1985; Muller, 1988; Sirowy and Inkeles, 1990; Gradstein and Milanovic, 2004; Mulligan et al., 2004; Scheve and Stasavage, 2009, 2010, 2012, 2017).

Controlling for the non-monotonic relationship between economic development and income inequality, Bollen and Grandjean (1981) do not find significant evidence in a sample of 50 countries to support the M-R hypothesis. Bollen and Jackman (1985) construct a simultaneous equation model that accounts for reciprocal interaction between political democracy and income inequality. Still, they do not find evidence of the direct effects of political democracy (Bollen's index of political democracy) on income inequality (World Bank database), or vice versa. However, they conclude that economic development influences both variables (political democracy and income inequality), while world-system position (Protestantism and British colonial experience) affects political democracy. Controlling for the level of economic development, Muller (1988) tests the effects of the duration of democratic experience on inequality using Bollen's political democracy index. Muller finds that a minimum of 20 years of democratic experience is necessary before the equalizing effects of democracy emerge. In other words, regardless of the level of economic development, democracy must be sustained for a significant period before it can reduce income inequality. Using the *Luxembourg Income Study* dataset (24 countries observed over 40 years, from 1967 to 2006), Scervini (2012) does not find a significant relationship between democracy and redistribution. Not only are the gains from redistribution negligible for the middle class, but the link between income and redistribution is also weaker for the middle class than for other income classes. In a more recent empirical study, Acemoglu et al. (2015) create 1- and 5-year panels for 184 countries, from independence or 1960 through 2010, but still fail to produce results that support the M-R hypothesis. Specifically, they do not find consistent evidence of a significant effect of democracy on equality. Examining the effects of political institutions on fiscal redistribution for a country-level panel from 1960 to 2010, Kammas and Sarantides (2019) assert that non-democratic regimes achieve significantly greater direct fiscal redistribution than democratic ones.

There are some studies that support the M-R hypothesis. Rodrik (1999) demonstrates a positive correlation between democracy and the level of manufacturing wages. Controlling for labor productivity, income levels, and other possible determinants for the period 1946–1994, Rodrik finds a robust and statistically significant relationship between the extent of democracy and the level of manufacturing wages across countries, as well as over time within countries. For 62 countries for 1965–1975, Simpson (1990) concludes that inequality maximizes at an intermediate level of democracy, reporting an inverted-U curve.

3.2.2 *Robin Hood Paradox*

Numerous empirical studies have been unable to definitively establish a direct link between democracy, income inequality, and redistributive policies. Interestingly, some empirical evidence contradicts the M-R model. In cross-national comparisons, researchers have observed the *Robin Hood Paradox*, which suggests that redistribution is more successful in relatively more equal countries than in nations with higher income inequality (Iversen and Soskice, 2009).

Figure 3.4 illustrates the relationship between wage inequality (ratio of the 9th and 5th percentiles) and income redistribution (difference between pre-tax Gini and post-tax Gini) across 35 OECD countries from 2001 to 2016. The trend line's negative slope suggests a negative relationship, indicating that as pre-tax wage inequality decreases, income redistribution becomes more active. Thus, Figure 3.4 appears to support the *Robin Hood Paradox*, rather than the M-R hypothesis. Figure 3.5 replicates Figure 3.4, but with a different definition of redistribution. In this instance, redistribution is defined as the difference between pre-tax and post-tax poverty rates. This observation in Figure 3.5 further strengthens the notion of the *Robin Hood Paradox*. Upon analyzing both Figures 3.4 and 3.5, we find that countries with higher levels

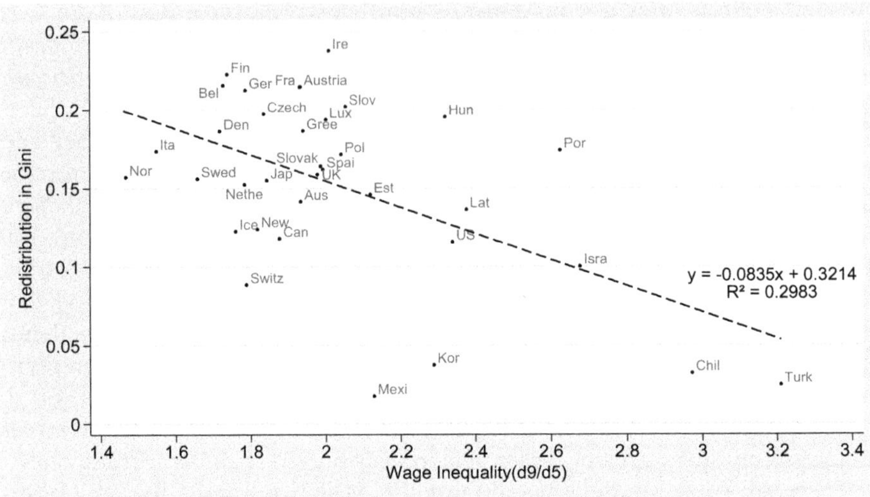

Figure 3.4 Robin Hood Paradox 1

Source: OECD databases.

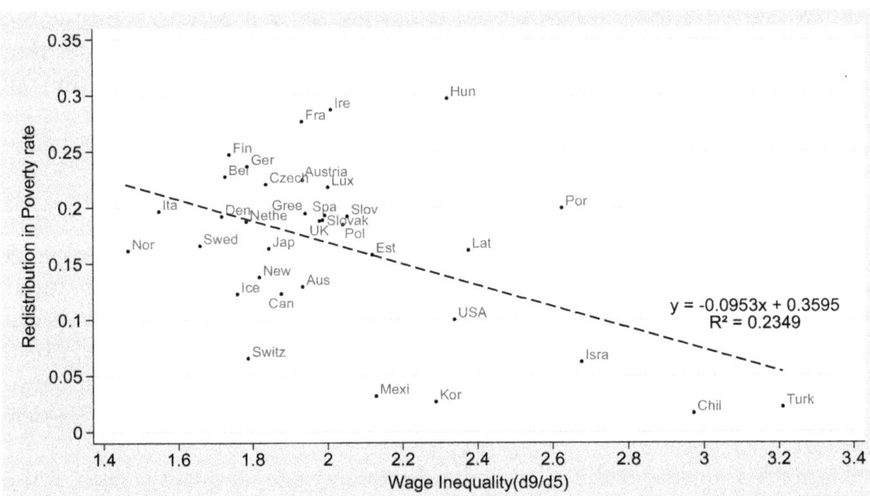

Figure 3.5 Robin Hood Paradox 2

Source: OECD databases.

of pre-tax wage income inequality tend to exhibit lower levels of redistribution. In contrast, countries with lower levels of pre-tax wage income inequality show more vigorous efforts in redistribution. Therefore, the study concludes that countries with lower inequality engage in more active redistribution policies, signifying the existence of the *Robin Hood Paradox*.

As a result, existing empirical research suggests that the relationship between democracy, income redistribution, and inequality is more complex than initially assumed by the M-R model. So, why does the expected outcome of the M-R model not materialize? One key factor to consider is that the M-R model lacks a comprehensive understanding of how escalating income inequality in the economic domain can undermine democracy and distort the political decision-making process. The M-R model optimistically assumes that the political domain, which emphasizes equality, can effectively regulate the economic domain, which fosters inequality. However, it fails to fully acknowledge that increasing income inequality in the economic domain can significantly shift the distribution of political power.

3.3 A preliminary explanation for the discrepancies between the predictions of the M-R model and reality

In this chapter, we have introduced the fundamental concepts of the M-R model and evaluated whether the model's predictions align with real-world outcomes, based on findings from previous empirical studies. Most of these empirical studies suggest that the anticipated equalizing effect of democracy has not been effectively realized, even in instances where income inequality has increased within democratic contexts. Chapter 4 explores various factors responsible for the gap between theoretical predictions and real-world outcomes. This examination is conducted using existing research and modeling methodologies. In this section, we concentrate on the model itself, specifically its assumptions, before the comprehensive analysis in Chapter 4. Within the model's assumptions framework, we aim to identify elements that contradict the M-R model's predictions, thereby uncovering potential reasons for the ineffectiveness of democracy's equalizing effect. Thus, this section can be viewed as a preliminary study conducted before the exploration in Chapter 4.

In simpler terms, as shown in Figure 3.6, ① represents the process proposed by the M-R model, where democracy ameliorates economic inequality. However, for this process to occur, the distribution of political power in the political domain must be more equitable than the income distribution in the economic domain. Regrettably, as depicted by ②, if income inequality leads to an uneven power distribution in the political domain, the M-R model's validity is undermined. Recognizing the importance of maintaining the political domain's

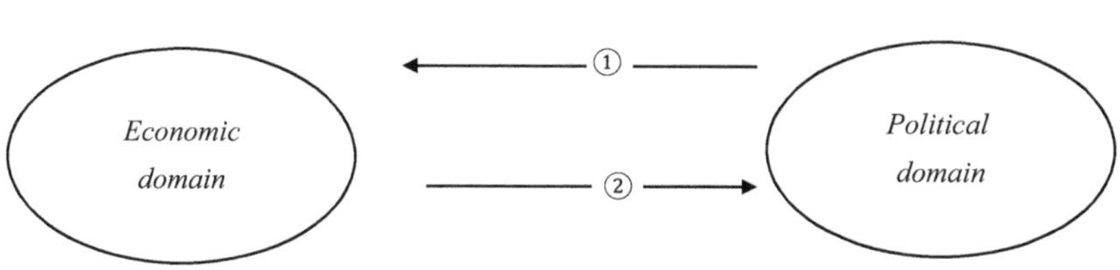

Figure 3.6 The factors that M-R overlooked

autonomy from the economic domain's influence, the M-R model posits the following two propositions.

M-R assumed that i) the distribution of voters by income level was skewed toward the lower-income level and that these lower-income voters would constitute the voting majority (refer to Figure 1.2). Given the political sector's principle of one person, one vote, M-R posited that lower-income voters would dominate the political arena. Moreover, they assumed that ii) political mechanisms exist to mediate the interests of lower-income groups.

Previous studies have shown that the M-R theory fails for several reasons. First, contrary to assumption i), if political power is unevenly distributed due to various factors, even in a democracy, redistribution efficiency will decline. For example, if the wealthy have invested in mechanisms (e.g., lobby and interest groups, collective action, threats to withdraw capital, media and ideological mobilization) to retain *de facto* political power in response to the expanded suffrage brought about by democratization or if policies that favor the rich gain social legitimacy, then the actual distribution of political power is no longer determined solely by voting numbers (compare Figures 1.2 and 1.4).[4] In this scenario, the decisive voter is no longer the middle-income class, but rather higher-income voters who have amassed real political power (Schattschneider, 1960; Gilens, 2005; Acemoglu and Robinson, 2008; Bartel, 2008; Hacker and Pierson, 2010; Stiglitz, 2012; Bresser-Pereira, 2014; Przeworski, 2014). In another scenario, if low-income individuals face voting obstacles, such as work commitments or regulations like pre-registration on voter rolls similar to the United States, and if voting rights are granted only to eligible voters who pass literacy and writing tests, the distribution of voters exercising their voting rights based on income level would shift to the right (indicated by the dotted line in Figure 3.7). As a result of reduced voter turnout among low-income individuals, the median income would also shift to the right. In simpler terms, as voting participation decreases among the extremely poor, including the low-income group, the distribution of actual voters exercising their voting rights would shift rightward, resulting in a shift from median income 1 to median income 2, as illustrated in Figure 3.7. Consequently, median income 2 necessitates a lower level of taxation, implying less redistribution compared to median income 1, resulting in a lower level of redistribution than initially anticipated. Second, if society's upper echelons encourage *privatization of conflict* to foster cleavages that benefit the higher-income class, the lower-income class will be divided by the ensuing cleavages, prompting lower-income voters to vote based on identity, rather than class (Schattschneider, 1960; Rodrik, 2014; Rodrik and Mukand, 2016). For example, if cleavages are established in society based on regional, religious, and racial or tribal conflict, then the voting-bloc unity of lower-income voters (who would otherwise constitute the majority) will be fragmented. If the lower- and higher-income classes share similar identities on issues related to regional, religious, and racial conflict, many lower-income voters will align with the higher-income class, resulting in *class betrayal voting* (see Figure 1.3). As a consequence, redistribution policies may not be enacted, even

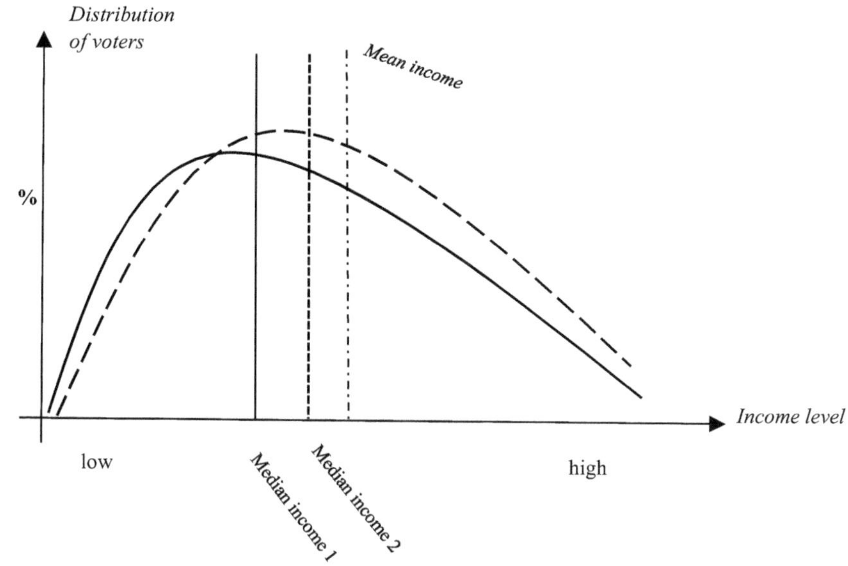

Figure 3.7 Low voter turnout rate among low-income voters

as income inequality escalates. Thirdly, M-R assume the political system can harmonize the interests of lower- and middle-income voters. However, in a two-party system without a party representing lower-income voters, only middle- and higher-income voters are represented by center-right and center-left parties, effectively disenfranchising lower-income voters (see Figure 3.8). Consequently, the low-income class remains marginalized, and their demands for redistribution policies are not effectively addressed. In countries where two

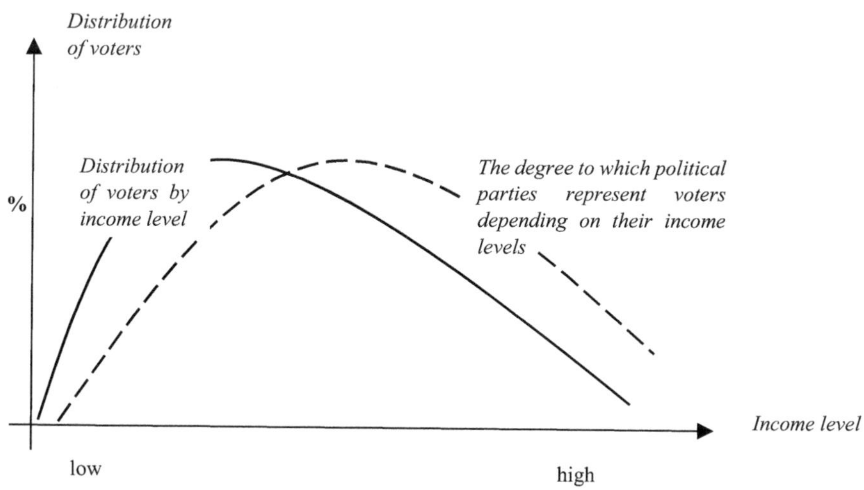

Figure 3.8 Inequality of representation

similar conservative centrist parties compete, they tend to cater to the conservative middle-class median voters who prefer less redistribution. As a result, even as income inequality intensifies, the proper implementation of income redistribution policies is obstructed (Hall and Soskice, 2001; Iversen and Soskice, 2009; Lijphart, 2012).

Notes

1 Akerlof and Kranton (2000) argue that preferences and interests are not formed externally, but rather, socially. A person's preferences and interests are determined by their perceived identity within society and how they justify this identity. Sen (2006) similarly posits that human interests are shaped, not only by structural or physical characteristics (e.g., gender, race, class), but also by social standards, morals, values, ideas, and other ideological factors. According to Akerlof and Kranton, individuals strive to belong to a certain societal group and emulate the societal standards of that specific group. If gender identity were considered a standard, there would be male and female categories in society, each with distinct diction, behavior, physical characteristics, clothing, and the like to represent the male and female standard, respectively.

2 For example, if a society composed of Christians, Hindus, and Muslims experiences identity cleavages due to religion, redistribution in the form of beef would result in members of individual religions experiencing different levels of post-redistribution income. Hindus, not consuming beef, would see a decline in post-tax income, while Christians and Muslims would experience no significant loss. Thus, a societal cleavage would emerge between Hindus, who abstain from beef, and Christians and Muslims, who consume beef. However, if redistribution occurs in the form of pork, Christians and Hindus would not oppose this, but Muslims would. This would create a cleavage between Christians and Hindus against Muslims.

3 The concept of democracy here follows the somewhat relaxed definition of Acemoglu and Robinson (2006), where democracy is defined based on political equality and rule by the majority, rather than Tilly (2007) or Dahl's (1998) definitions, which are based on the relationships between nation and citizen or on procedural justice. Political equality is understood as the condition where the majority's preferences and interests are fairly represented in society, while political inequality is defined as a situation where the preferences and interests of the elite are overrepresented.

4 Zingales (2017) highlights that the elite's ability to capture *de facto* political power through investment is evidence of the imperfection of contracts, rules, and laws. If imperfections in contracts, rules, and laws are not entirely eliminated through prior regulation, the possibility persists that those with disproportionate power can intervene in the distribution of economic rent. Zingales posits that the elite invest in *de facto* political power mechanisms because they anticipate the increased rent distribution gains from influencing political, legal, and regulatory systems to outweigh the costs of those investments. Zingales refers to the cycle wherein wealth generates political power and political power produces wealth as the *Medici vicious circle*.

References

Acemoglu, D., S. Naidu, P. Restrepo, and J. A. Robinson (2015), "Democracy, redistribution, and inequality," In Atkinson, A. B. and F. Bourguignon(eds), *Handbook of Income Distribution*, Vol. 2, pp. 1885–1966, Amsterdam: Elsevier.

Acemoglu, D. and J. Robinson (2012), *Why nations fail: The origins of power, prosperity, and poverty*, New York: Crown Business.
Acemoglu, D. and J. Robinson (2008), "Persistence of power, elites, and institutions," *American Economic Review*, Vol. 98, No. 1, pp. 267–269.
Acemoglu, D. and J. Robinson (2006), *Economic Origins of Dictatorship and Democracy*, New York: Cambridge University Press.
Akerlof, G. A. and R. E. Kranton (2000), "Economics and identity," *Quarterly Journal of Economics*, Vol. 115, No. 3, pp. 715–753.
Bartels, L. (2008), *Unequal democracy: The political economy of the new gilded age*, Princeton: Princeton University.
Bassett, W., J. Burkett, and L. Putterman (1999), "Income distribution, government transfers, and problem of unequal influence," *European Journal of Political Economy*, Vol. 15, No. 2, pp. 207–228.
Berle, A. and G. Means (1932), *Modern Corporation and Private Property*, New Brunswick and London: Transaction Publishers.
Bollen, K. and B. Grandjean (1981), "The dimension(s) of democracy: further issues in the measurement and effects of political democracy," *American Sociological Review*, Vol. 46, No. 5, pp. 651–659.
Bollen, K. and R. Jackman (1985), "Political democracy and the size distribution of income," *American Sociological Review*, Vol. 50, No. 4, pp. 438–457.
Bresser-Pereira, L. C. (2014), "The hegemony constraints in the neoliberal years of capitalism," in Magara, E. (ed), *Economic crises and policy regimes*, pp. 56–78, Cheltenham: Edward Elgar Publishing Limited.
Dahl, R. A. (1998), *On Democracy*, New Haven: Yale University Press.
Downs, A. (1957), *An economic theory of democracy*, New York: Harper and Row Publishers.
Gilens, M. (2005), "Inequality and democratic responsiveness," *Public Opinion Quarterly*, Vol. 69, No. 5, pp. 778–796.
Gradstein, M. and B. Milanovic (2004), "Does liberté = egalité? A survey of the empirical links between democracy and inequality with some evidence on the transition economies," *Journal of Economic Surveys*, Vol. 18, No. 4, pp. 515–537.
Hacker, J. and P. Pierson (2010), *Winner-take-all politics: How Washington made the rich richer and turned its back on the middle class*, New York: Simon & Schuster Paperbacks.
Hall, P. A. and D. Soskice (2001), *Varieties of capitalism: The institutional foundations of comparative advantage*, Oxford: Oxford University Press.
Iversen, T. and D. Soskice (2009), "Distribution and redistribution: The shadow of the nineteenth century," *World Politics*, Vol. 61, No. 3, pp. 438–486.
Kammas, P. and V. Sarantides (2019), "Do dictatorships redistribute more?," *Journal of Comparative Economics*, Vol. 47, No. 1, pp. 176–195.
Lijphart, A. (2012), *Patterns of democracy: Government forms and performance in thirty-six countries*, New Heaven: Yale University Press.
Meltzer, A. H. and S. F. Richard (1981), "A rational theory of the size of government," *Journal of Political Economy*, Vol. 89, No. 5, pp. 914–927.
Milanovic, B. (2010), "Four critiques of the redistribution hypothesis: An assessment," *European Journal of Political Economy*, Vol. 26, No. 1, pp. 147–154.
Muller, E. (1988), "Democracy, economic development, and income inequality," *American Sociological Review*, Vol. 53, No. 1, pp. 50–68.
Mulligan, C. B., R. Gil, and X. Sala-i-Martin (2004), "Do democracies have different public policies than non-democracies?" *Journal of Economic Perspectives*, Vol. 18, No. 1, pp. 51–74.
Okun, A. M. (1975), *Equality and efficiency: The big trade-off*, Washington, DC: Brooking Institution Press.

Perotti, R. (1996), "Growth, income distribution, and democracy: what the data say," *Journal of Economic Growth*, Vol. 1, No. 2, pp. 149–187.

Przeworski, A. (2014), "Choices and echoes: Stability and change of policy regimes," in Magara, E. (ed), *Economic crises and policy regimes*, pp 33–55, Cheltenham: Edward Elgar Publishing Limited.

Rodrik, D. (2014), "When ideas trump interests: Preferences, worldviews, and policy innovations," *Journal of Economic Perspectives*, Vol. 28, No. 1, pp. 189–208.

Rodrik, D. (1999), "Democracies pay higher wages," *Quarterly Journal of Economics*, Vol. 114, No. 3, pp. 707–738.

Rodrik, D. and S. Mukand (2016), "Ideas versus interests: A unified political economy framework," http://j.mp/2ovA6Zu

Romer, T. (1975), "Individual welfare, majority voting, and the properties of a linear income tax," *Journal of Public Economics*, Vol. 4, No. 2, pp. 163–185.

Schattschneider, E. E. (1960), *The semi-sovereign people: A realist view of democracy in America*, New York: Holt, Rinehart and Winston.

Scervini, F. (2012), "Empirics of the median voter: democracy, redistribution and the role of middle class," *Journal of Economic Inequality*, Vol. 10, No. 4, pp. 529–550.

Scheve, K. and Stasavage, D. (2017), "Wealth inequality and democracy," *Annual Review of Political Science*, Vol. 20, pp. 451–468.

Scheve, K. and Stasavage, D. (2012), "Democracy, war, and wealth: Lessons from two centuries of inheritance taxation," *American Political Science Review*, Vol. 106, No. 1, pp. 82–102.

Scheve, K. and Stasavage, D. (2010), "The conscription of wealth: Mass warfare and the demand for progressive taxation," *International Organization*, Vol. 64, No. 4, pp. 529–561.

Scheve, K. and Stasavage, D. (2009), "Institutions, partisanship, and inequality in the long run," *World Politics*, Vol. 61, No. 2, pp. 215–253.

Sen, A. (2006), *Identity and violence: The illusion of destiny*, New York: W.W.W. Norton.

Simpson, M. (1990), "Political rights and income inequality: a cross-national test," *American Sociological Review*, Vol. 55, No. 5, pp. 682–693.

Sirowy, L. and A. Inkeles (1990), "The effects of democracy on economic growth and inequality: A review," *Studies in Comparative International Development*, Vol. 25, No. 1, pp. 126–157.

Stiglitz, J. E. (2012), *The price of inequality: How today's divided society endangers our future*, New York: W.W. Norton & Company.

Tilly, C. (2007), *Democracy*, New York: Cambridge University Press.

Waldfogel, J. (2001), "The deadweight loss of Christmas," *American Economic Review*, Vol. 83, No. 5, pp. 1328–1336.

Zingales, L. (2017), "Towards a political theory of the firm," *Journal of Economic Perspectives*, Vol. 31, No. 3, pp. 113–130.

4 Why has the M-R hypothesis failed to materialize in democratic nations?

Chapter 3 explored the reasons why democracy struggles to achieve income redistribution, focusing specifically on the limitations of the M-R model's hypotheses. In this chapter, our aim is to examine why the M-R hypothesis, which suggests that income redistribution policies would be more vigorously implemented as income inequality increases, does not align well with democratic countries. To do this, we will scrutinize the policy-making process, where the economic and political domains interact, and provide an explanation. Therefore, the approach adopted in Chapter 3, centered around the M-R model's hypothesis, and the approach taken in Chapter 4, focusing on the dynamic process of policy formulation, are expected to offer complementary perspectives that illuminate the reasons behind the unfulfilled realization of the M-R hypothesis in democracy.

4.1 Political economy of income redistribution

The influence of political factors on economic performance has been a long-standing subject of inquiry within both the economic and political fields. With the issue of income inequality gaining increased global attention recently, the relationship between democracy and income inequality is once again under scrutiny. Building on previous research conducted by Downs (1957) and Romer (1975), M-R (Meltzer and Richard, 1981) argued that democracy promotes economic equality. According to the M-R hypothesis, as the majority of citizens are enfranchised in a democracy, greater income inequality leads to public support for income redistribution policies, which can help mitigate income inequality. However, when examining the trends of democratization and income inequality since the 1990s, we find that the two variables have been moving in opposite directions, contrary to the predictions made by the M-R hypothesis. The *Global Report on Conflict, Governance, and State Fragility*, authored by Marshall and Elzinga-Marshall (2017), revealed that over the past 20–30 years, South American and Eastern bloc countries have undergone a rapid transition from autocratic regimes to more open governance. As a result, the number of democratic nations worldwide has nearly doubled, increasing from 48 in 1989 to 99 as of 2018 (Figure 4.1). In contrast, income

DOI: 10.4324/9781032695754-4

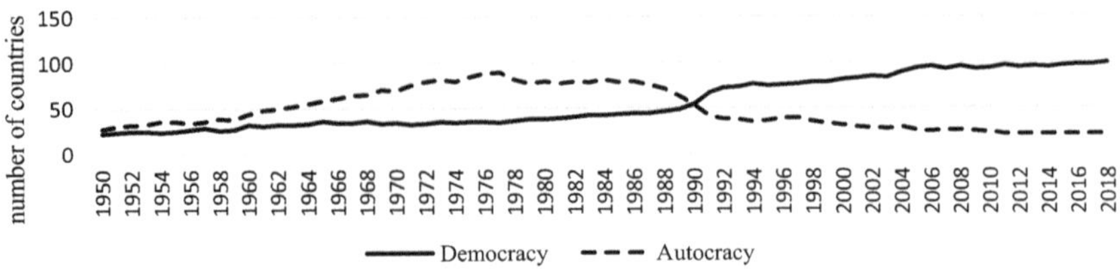

Figure 4.1 Global trends in governance, 1950–2018

Source: Marshall and Gurr (2020), *Polity V project, political regime characteristics and transitions, 1800–2018*, Vienna, VA: Center for Systemic Peace.

inequality has risen in nearly all regions since 1980, according to the World Inequality Lab's *World Inequality Report 2018* (2017), although the rates of increase in income inequality have varied by country and region. Over the past 40 years, income inequality has increased rapidly in North America, China, India, and Russia, while in Europe, income inequality has been trending upward at a relatively slower pace. Consequently, despite the global increase in the number of democratic countries over the past four decades, income inequality has also risen. Therefore, considering these experiences of the past 40 years, it is challenging to find clear evidence supporting the M-R assertion that democratization alleviates income inequality. In fact, many empirical studies (Sirowy and Inkeles, 1990; Gradstein and Milanovic, 2004; Mulligan et al., 2004; Scheve and Stasavage, 2009, 2010, 2012) have failed to establish a clear link between democracy, income inequality, and redistribution policies. Furthermore, certain results, referred to as the *Robin Hood Paradox*, are even contrary to the M-R hypothesis. They suggest that redistribution occurs more effectively in more egalitarian countries and that unequal societies engage in even less redistribution (Iversen and Soskice, 2009).

4.1.1 Interaction between the political and economic domains

As numerous empirical studies do not support the M-R hypothesis, researchers have turned their attention toward investigating the reasons responsible for the M-R hypothesis not coming to fruition within democratic countries. In the preceding chapter, we underscored the limitations associated with the assumptions underpinning the M-R model. In this chapter, we introduce the domain of political-economic interaction, where politics and economics converge to shape policies related to income redistribution. Building on this foundation, our aim is to provide a systematic explanation for the challenges in implementing the M-R hypothesis in democratic nations. Moreover, we aim to clarify how existing research relates to various aspects of this complex political-economic domain.

Figure 4.2 presents the central assertion of this study, illustrating how the economic and political domains interact to shape policies and influence economic performance. Figure 4.2 will be used to explain why the equalizing effects of democracy do not function effectively in democratic countries.

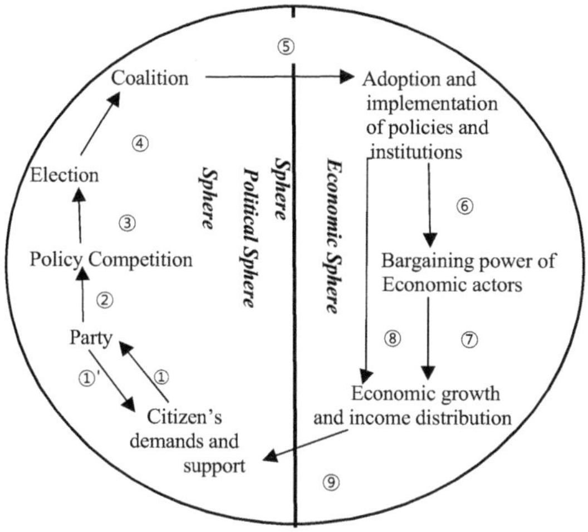

Figure 4.2 The dynamic interaction between the political and economic domains, and the M-R hypothesis

Source: Boyer (2014), p. 132.

In the above figure, the left side represents the political domain, illustrating how citizens' demands and support drive the policy formation of political parties. Additionally, it demonstrates how alliances are established based on elections and policies. The right side of the figure represents the economic domain. It illustrates how policies and institutions established in the political domain impact the bargaining power of different socio-economic groups and influence economic performance, including growth and distribution.

A further explanation of the above is as follows. Political parties create policies in response to the demands of citizens (① and ②), compete in elections based on these policies (③), and form political coalitions based on the election results (④). The political coalition that gains power then selects policies and institutions according to their own interests (⑤). Indeed, the government's ability to enforce these political decisions in the economic domain plays a crucial role. The policies and institutions put in place impact technological advancements in the economic domain, the supply of factors of production, the bargaining power of economic actors, and the relative prices of factors of production (⑥ and ⑧). Consequently, the pattern of economic growth and income distribution in a society is established (⑦ and ⑧). Moreover, these economic achievements trigger a new political cycle by creating support among citizens for individual political parties and leading to the emergence of new political demands (⑨).

4.1.2 Previous research on the invalidation of the M-R hypothesis

The M-R hypothesis provides a linear explanation for the occurrence of redistribution when income inequality increases, based on the median voter theory, without considering the complex political process illustrated in Figure 4.2. However, the demand from citizens for redistribution often leads to a result that differs from the initial intention, as it is refracted and distorted through this complex political process. Indeed, the differences in political systems that govern this complex political process significantly impact the outcome of redistribution across different countries.

Drawing from Figure 4.2, we review previous research findings that explain why the M-R hypothesis does not hold in democratic countries. We analyze how these findings relate to different aspects of Figure 4.2. Using Figure 4.2 as a framework, we aim to compare and synthesize various existing studies.

The first explanation for why the M-R hypothesis is not realized in democratic countries is the *captured democracy hypothesis* (Stiglitz, 2012). In studies on American democracy, a significant focus is on the issues of voice and listening inequality between different social groups. Political scientists in the United States often emphasize the concept of pluralistic polyarchy, where numerous interest groups compete for influence. However, as astutely stated by Schattschneider (1960), a flaw in this pluralistic paradise is that the voices of the upper class resonate more loudly in the political discourse. Due to the frequent and effective expression of opinions by the affluent compared to other income groups, the political system tends to be more responsive to the interests of the wealthy. Consequently, the wealthy tend to be *overrepresented* despite being a numerical minority, while the demands for income redistribution from low-income groups often become *underrepresented* in the political domain, resulting in an increase in political inequality (Bartel, 2008; Hacker and Pierson, 2010; Stiglitz, 2012; Acemoglu et al., 2013). This phenomenon of underrepresentation among low-income groups is also linked to their low voter turnout. In the United States, for example, voter turnout among the busy, impoverished individuals barely reaches 50%, while nine out of ten affluent individuals participate in voting.[1] The low voter turnout within the low-income group can be attributed to their limited availability and high illiteracy rates. For instance, in the United States, regulations such as mandatory pre-registration before elections or restrictions that limit voting rights to citizens who pass literacy tests for reading and writing contribute to this situation.

Acemoglu et al. and Schattschneider highlight the increasing inequality in the representation process and provide insights into why the M-R hypothesis is not upheld. They emphasize the need to distinguish between the *de jure* political power defined by the law and the *de facto* political power actually held by different income groups, which they term *captured democracy*. According to their analysis, the affluent class actively seeks *de facto* political power through various means, such as lobbying for political influence, contributing to campaign funds, establishing influential networks to shape public opinion, and using the threat of capital flight overseas. On the other hand, the middle- and low-income groups experience a rapid decline in their *de facto* political power, paralleling the weakening of labor unions that traditionally represented their interests and the widening income inequality. Consequently, the affluent class, equipped with megaphones, effectively raises its demands during the policy-making process of political parties. Meanwhile, the low-income group, with muted voices, finds their calls for income redistribution largely overlooked and insufficiently addressed by the political system. As a result, the equalizing effects of democracy fail to fully materialize, as evidenced by these explanations.

The captured democracy hypothesis highlights the distortion in the process of ① and ② in Figure 4.2, wherein the voices of the affluent class are overrepresented in party and policy-making. In particular, Schattschneider (1960) draws attention to the disparity between the policies promised by politicians to citizens before elections and the policies they ultimately support and vote for after elections. He is particularly interested in scenarios where citizens lack the means to compel politicians to fulfill the promises they made before elections, referred to as *semi-sovereign people.* In such situations, instead of working to fulfill their promises, politicians often favor the interests of the affluent class that lobbied for them, leading to the establishment of a sponsor–beneficiary structure. Even if political parties gain power based on their commitment to income redistribution, the politicians in office may yield to the pressures of lobbying from the affluent class or interest groups, supporting policies that benefit them rather than strictly adhering to the mandate given by the citizens. This sponsorship–beneficiary structure creates a discrepancy between the income redistribution policies promised by the parties before elections and the policies they actually endorse and vote for afterward, making the realization of the M-R hypothesis challenging.

The second explanation centers on how income redistribution issues are weakened through the *privatization of conflict* or *class betrayal voting* (Schattschneider, 1960). Lipset–Rokkan's cleavage theory (1967) posits that Western European democracies developed distinct party systems through cleavages like center/periphery, state/church, city/rural, and capital/labor, which overlapped and varied across countries. In contrast, Schattschneider's theory suggests that in the United States and developing countries, with shorter democratic histories, parties and elites selectively employ and exclude different cleavage factors, leading to diverse party systems and voter distributions. He observes that, whereas cleavage led to the formation of political parties in Western European democracies, the United States and developing countries experienced a *privatization of conflict*, where parties and political elites privately mobilize and exploit cleavages. Established dominant political coalitions strive to preserve their alliances by consistently leveraging the conflicts that emerge from these cleavages. In contrast, aspiring competitive political coalitions adopt a strategy of alternative conflict, mobilizing different cleavages. They also exploit potential conflicts within the dominant coalition to fragment it. The essence of this strategy involves introducing new conflicts that supplant existing ones. For example, the Democratic Party ascended to power by emphasizing economic cleavages following the New Deal policies, while the Republican Party gained power in 1972 by highlighting alternative conflicts such as race, welfare, crime, and resistance movements. In this interpretation, political parties disadvantaged in redistribution issues adopt a strategy of dividing the middle class and low-income groups, who share a common perspective on redistribution. Rather than focusing on income inequality and redistribution, they exploit new cleavages (e.g., abortion, regional, security, religious, and gender issues) to create divisions within the middle- and low-income groups. As a result, demands for redistribution are diluted, and the internal unity of the middle- and low-income groups is fractured. Political parties shift their policy competition from redistribution-related issues to new cleavage issues. Consequently, despite a rise in income inequality, the need for and demands for redistribution may increase, but the policy focus on redistribution becomes diluted.[2] The privatization of conflict hypothesis elucidates that the distortion depicted in '①' of Figure 4.2 is the fundamental reason why it is difficult for the equalizing effect of democracy to be properly realized in democratic countries.

The third pathway is elucidated by the concept of *policy regime* proposed by Przeworski (2014) and Bresser-Pereira (2014). A policy regime denotes a state of strategic equilibrium where different parties, despite having distinct ideologies and support bases, propose and implement similar policies.[3] During a specific policy regime, political parties do not compete over alternative policies despite ideological differences. Instead, they perceive the dominant policy set as the *one best way* and concentrate on implementing it more efficiently. Consequently, regardless of which party assumes power, they end up adopting similar policies. Moreover, successful cases in certain countries lead to global policy convergence through imitation or under the pressure of international organizations, as seen in East Asian countries after the foreign exchange crisis.

Post World War II, the Keynesian and neoliberal policy regimes serve as illustrative examples. For instance, during the Fordism era with Keynesian economics, the belief in managing economic fluctuations through demand manipulation or active government intervention in market failures gained widespread agreement across parties, resulting in the adoption of similar policies and establishing historical precedents for policy regimes. In the post-1980s era of the neoliberal policy regime, the belief that markets can maximize welfare and efficiency without extensive government intervention led both left- and right-wing parties to implement policy sets involving privatization, reduced government debt and social security expenditure, and market liberalization with minimal government interference.

While Bresser-Pereira concurs with Przeworski's definition of a policy regime, he actively incorporates Gramsci's concept of hegemony, unlike Przeworski, who emphasizes Bayesian learning in the formation of policy regimes. During an economic crisis that casts doubt on the validity of the existing policy regime, various political coalitions vie for dominance, offering diverse analyses and solutions. These political alliances diagnose the current crisis, propose alternatives, and present solutions, seeking societal support. If they secure societal backing for their diagnosis, alternatives, and solutions, the policy set they propose is recognized as legitimate, leading to the establishment of a new policy regime. The political coalitions that advocate for and support this new policy regime become the dominant political alliances. Having secured societal consent and legitimacy for their policy set, they fully exercise the ideological hegemony advocated by Gramsci and Bourdieu. Consequently, when a policy regime exercises ideological hegemony, as described by Przeworski, political parties choose similar policies despite their ideological differences.[4] During the era of the neoliberal policy regime, proponents contended that reducing corporate taxes and social security expenditures were necessary to boost business competitiveness and stimulate investment, leading to a trickle-down effect that would benefit society as a whole. This justification conferred social legitimacy to the neoliberal policy regime. As a result, if the neoliberal policy regime secured societal approval, regardless of which political party assumed power, there would be a passive approach to implementing redistributive policies (as indicated in Figure 4.2 by the arrow from party to policy competition, ②). When the dominant political coalition exercises ideological hegemony, redistributive policies that pose a threat to the interests of the dominant coalition are actively obstructed, regardless of election outcomes (as depicted in Figure 4.2 by the arrow from election results to coalition, ③ and ④). Consequently, redistributive policies that challenge the interests of the dominant coalition are not vigorously pursued, as depicted in Figure 4.2 by the arrow from coalition to policy and institutional adoption and implementation (⑤).

The fourth explanation pertains to *government capacity*, with a particular emphasis on transparency and trust in the government. Rothstein (2005) argues that the high levels of social capital in Nordic countries are not solely a result of the development of social networks, as suggested by Putnam (1993), but rather originate from the transparency and trust in the government. Similarly, Hetherington (2004) points out that the weakening of public policies in the United States is linked to the decline in trust in the government. Both scholars highlight that countries with significant redistribution and extensive welfare expenditures often exhibit higher levels of citizen trust in government transparency. Therefore, when the government becomes opaque and corrupt, leading to widespread distrust, citizens may resist high taxation or engage in tax evasion (Rothstein, 2005). As a result, even in the face of increasing income inequality, citizens may favor lower tax rates and a smaller government, leading to diminished redistributive measures (depicted in the process of ⑧ in Figure 4.2).

The fifth explanation explores *the interaction between electoral systems, political systems, and redistributive policies*, drawing on Lijphart's (2012) cross-national comparative analysis of political systems and Hall and Soskice's (2001) discussion on the variety of capitalism. They emphasize that redistributive policies emerge from the political system, where resources are allocated through political processes, separate from market-based resource allocation. They categorize democratic political systems into two primary models: majoritarian and proportional representation. The majoritarian model adopts a 'winner-takes-all' approach, where only the top candidate with the most votes in each constituency secures a seat, and it is typically associated with single-member and two-party systems. In contrast, the proportional representation or consensus model allocates legislative seats in proportion to party vote shares and is associated with nationwide multi-member districts and multi-party systems. Consequently, the outcomes of redistributive policies are shaped by the electoral system and the subsequent formation of political coalitions.

Iversen and Soskice's (2009) model delves into the correlation between electoral systems and income redistribution and welfare policies, suggesting that proportional representation electoral systems are more supportive of such policies compared to majoritarian systems. Coalition formation differences between majoritarian and proportional representation systems influence the nature of the ruling party (right-wing or left-wing coalition), thereby impacting variations in redistributive and social policies. An analysis of 17 advanced countries from 1945 to 1998 revealed that proportional representation systems tend to foster left-wing coalition governments, which are more inclined toward income redistribution and welfare policies. The model takes into account three social strata (low-income, middle-class, and wealthy) and two electoral systems (majoritarian/proportional representation). Rational choice theory suggests that the middle class plays a crucial role in determining which party ascends to power. The middle class can align with either the low-income stratum to tax the wealthy or with the wealthy to prevent higher taxation by the low-income stratum. However, in a majoritarian two-party system, only center-right parties representing the wealthy and center-left parties representing the low-income class exist, leaving no centrist party to represent the middle class. The middle class tends to support right-wing parties that favor low tax rates, as they lack assurance and trust that left-wing parties will implement policies imposing high taxes solely on the wealthy, excluding themselves, once they gain power. In contrast, under a proportional representation system, the existence of a centrist party representing the middle class encourages trust and cooperation with left-wing parties. The centrist party collaborates with left-wing parties to impose taxes on the wealthy and implement redistributive policies that benefit both the low-income and middle-class strata. As a result, left-wing parties are more likely to gain power through coalitions with centrist parties under proportional representation systems. They also tend to be more proactive in adopting redistributive and welfare policies to address the needs of the lower- and middle-income strata.[5]

Iversen and Soskice concentrate on the impact of electoral systems and political coalitions, investigating how the active implementation of redistributive policies becomes challenging under a multi-party system. However, scholars such as Seon (2015) and Choi (2010) propose various additional pathways that obstruct income redistribution policies under a majoritarian-two-party, single-district system. In this system, parties tend to prioritize the preferences of the median voter, leading to minimal policy differentiation and a failure to represent the interests and values of diverse groups and classes on both sides of the median voter. The policy content varies based on the identity and preferred policies of the median voter. If the median voter does not favor high taxation and shares a similar identity (values and beliefs) with the high-income stratum, major parties are less likely to adopt redistributive or welfare policies. Choi posits that in countries like South Korea, where ideological constraints persist due to division and the Cold War, a political agency system dominated by conservative forces prevails. As a result, both conservative parties perceive median voters as those who support ***anti-communism and economic development***, leading to a ***laborless democracy*** and a ***blind spot of representation*** where the interests and demands of citizens and labor classes are not politically represented. Seon further argues that under a political system that combines majority and two-party systems, politicians are preoccupied with local interest issues, making them less proactive in implementing redistributive and welfare policies directly related to various strata and groups, especially the low-income class. In contrast, under a multi-party system, each party represents the understanding and values of the groups and classes supporting them, reducing the representation blind spot, and showing more interest in universal social policies.

Therefore, in the context of Figure 4.2, electoral systems and political institutions influence policy competition and election outcomes (③), as well as the content and feasibility of political coalitions (④).[6] Naturally, if political coalitions consist of groups and classes favoring redistributive policies, more proactive income redistribution and welfare policies will be adopted, leading to an improvement in income redistribution.

The focus on political institutions may lead to the Robin Hood Paradox within the political institution matrix of a majoritarian-two-party, single-district system. Here, income inequality may increase due to insufficient allocation of political resources for redistributive policies or welfare programs. Conversely, advocates of another political institution matrix, the proportional representation-multi-party-multi-district, argue that it is more conducive to social policy outcomes, such as redistributive and welfare policies.

Referring to Figure 4.2, we present the outcomes of previous research on why the M-R hypothesis is not realized within democratic systems. However, beyond these explanations, there exist additional hypotheses. The skewed perceptions of income distribution and the prospect of upward mobility serve as supplementary explanations. Crues et al. (2013) found, through analyzing data from a 2009 Argentinian survey, that a significant factor contributing to the failure of democratic societies to demand income redistribution—even in the face of increasing income inequality—is the systematic bias in people's perception of their own income ranking. A significant portion of individuals with lower income tend to overestimate their social standing, while a considerable number of individuals with higher income tend to underestimate their rank. This mechanism offers an alternative explanation for the inadequate levels of income redistribution observed in contemporary democracies. Conversely, Bénabou and Ok (2001) examine the impact of social mobility on the desire for redistribution. They propose that individuals with low income may resist high levels of redistribution if they believe they or their offspring have the potential to ascend the socio-economic ladder. The Prospect of Upward Mobility (POUM) hypothesis, a well-known theory, offers an explanation as to why most democratic societies refrain from practicing extensive expropriation or highly progressive redistribution.

Figure 4.2 illustrates the complex political procedure that income redistribution policies must navigate for their creation and implementation. While the M-R hypothesis imagines a straightforward democracy solely equipped with an electoral system, reality reveals potential for distortion or complexity in the policy formation process within a democratic context, as depicted in Figure 4.2. Therefore, considering the complex political process shown in Figure 4.2 and the interplay between the economic and political domains, the realization of the M-R hypothesis might be more of an exceptional event rather than a common occurrence.

From the aforementioned results, we can discern certain conditions that need to be cultivated to enhance income redistribution in a democracy. These conditions extend beyond the establishment of formal democratic institutions, such as a multi-party political system, universal adult suffrage, and regularly contested elections. Democratic societies must also effectively curb attempts by the wealthy to use their wealth to sway the political domain. Reducing discrimination based on race, religion, gender, and other factors is crucial. The electoral system must ensure a fair representation of the demands of different societal segments. Finally, it is essential to establish new policy regimes that can strike a balance between efficiency and equity.

4.2 Why does inequality not decline?

Building on the model discussed in Chapter 3, we delve into the reasons why the equalizing effect of democracy, as illustrated in the preceding Figure 4.2, fails to materialize.

4.2.1 Instances where the M-R model falls short

Case 1: Captured democracy

$$y_h = (1-t)a_h + \left(g - \frac{cg^2}{2} - \Gamma\right) \tag{4.1}$$

$$\Gamma = \beta g \tag{4.2}$$

$$y_m = a_m(1-t) \tag{4.3}$$

$$y_l = a_l(1-t) \tag{4.4}$$

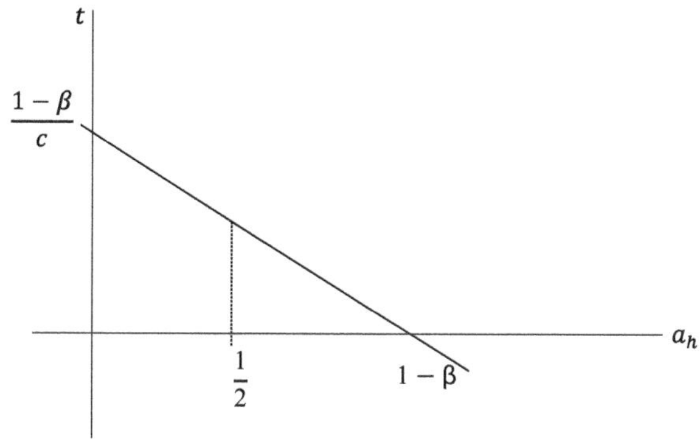

Figure 4.3 Captured democracy

We posit that the higher-income class pays a certain amount (Γ) (Equation 4.1) to manipulate the political system, and that Γ escalates as the anticipated magnitude of redistribution (g) increases. In essence, we assume $\Gamma = \beta g$ (Equation 4.2), and that the tax burden is shared across all three classes (Equations 4.1, 4.3, and 4.4). The tax rate is dictated by the higher-income class, which has broadened its political sway. By substituting the balanced budget constraint ($g = t$) into Equation 4.1 and solving for the tax rate (t_c) that optimizes higher-income class disposable income, we derive the following:

$$t_c = \frac{1 - a_h - \beta}{c} \tag{4.5}$$

Figure 4.3 depicts a captured democracy scenario where, because a_h is larger than $\frac{1}{2}$, β is less than $\frac{1}{2}$. The closer a_h is to $\frac{1}{2}$, or the relatively lower the is market income of the higher-income class, the more tax rates will increase to distribute more wealth to the higher-income class.

Case 2: Policy regime: Favoring the higher-income class

If the redistribution of wealth to the higher-income class (or subsidies to corporations within the higher-income class) can be justified and accepted by the lower- and middle-income classes, then, unlike in a captured democracy, the higher-income class can set the tax rate at its preferred level and redistribute wealth to itself without incurring additional costs to justify these policies. Therefore, under this scenario, we assume $\Gamma = 0$ (equation 4.6).

$$y_h = (1-t)a_h + g - \frac{cg^2}{2} \tag{4.6}$$

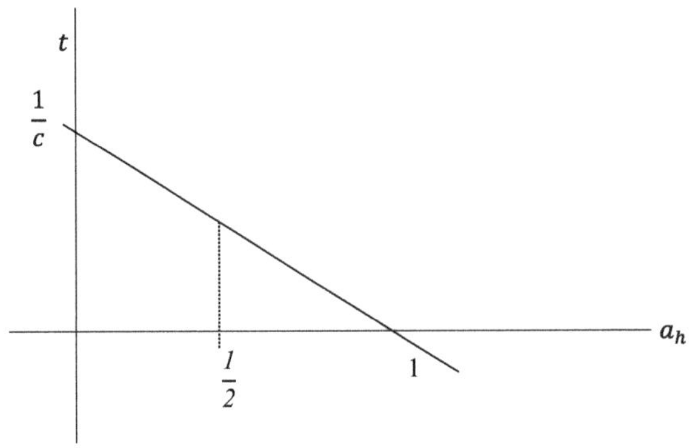

Figure 4.4 Policy regime favoring the higher-income class

Under a policy regime favoring the higher-income class, such as neoliberalism, the tax rate (t_{pr}) that maximizes the disposable income of the higher-income class is as follows:

$$t_{pr} = \frac{1 - a_h}{c} \tag{4.7}$$

Figure 4.4 illustrates the equation under a policy regime where the market income of the higher-income class (a_h) falls between $\frac{1}{2}$ and 1. In this scenario, the closer a_h is to ½, or the lower is the income of the higher-income class, the higher the tax rate imposed to redistribute wealth to the wealthy.

Case 3: Corrupt government

Corruption in government also leads to greater leakage during redistribution, increasing c in Equation 4.5. In this instance, the M-R model must be adjusted to accommodate these changes, as follows, where $c' > c$.

$$y_m = a_m(1-t) + n_1 g - \frac{c' g^2}{2} n_1 \tag{4.8}$$

$$y_l = a_l(1-t) + n_2 g - \frac{c' g^2}{2} n_2 \tag{4.9}$$

The tax rate (t_{tr}) established under a corrupt and nontransparent government is lower than the tax rate (t_{mr}) under M-R, reflecting the relatively inefficient income redistribution.

$$t_{tr} = \frac{n_1 - a_m}{c' n_1} < \frac{n_1 - a_m}{c n_1} = t_{mr} \tag{4.10}$$

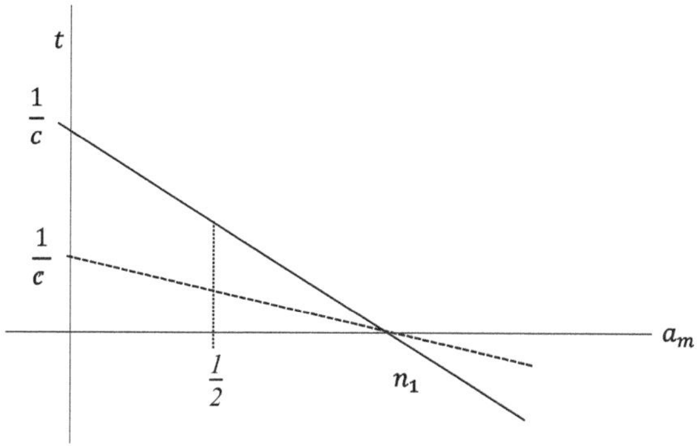

Figure 4.5 Corrupt government

Figure 4.5 depicts the outcome under a corrupt government. Compared to the M-R scenario (solid line), c increases to c' when the government is corrupt (indicated by a dashed line). In this situation, given the same degree of inequality, voters prefer lower tax rates under a corrupt government than they would under a clean government.

Case 4: Absence of a political party capable of representing the interests of the lower-income class under a two-party system

The M-R model assumes the existence of a political mechanism to coordinate the interests of the lower- and middle-income classes. However, when only two parties exist to represent the middle- and higher-income voters and lower-income voters lack a party voice, as described in the Iversen and Soskice (2009) model, the analysis arrives at a different conclusion than that reached under the M-R model.[7]

Firstly, let's assume that neither the lower- nor higher-income classes individually hold an absolute majority, and each can only secure election victory with the support of the lower-income class (Equation 4.11):

$$n_m \left\langle \frac{1}{2},\ n_m + n_l \right\rangle \frac{1}{2},\ n_h + n_l > \frac{1}{2} \tag{4.11}$$

In this scenario, the lower-income class holds the deciding vote and can either advocate for income redistribution by supporting the middle-class party or endorse lower taxes by backing the higher-income class party. However, the lower-income class faces a trust issue when considering voting for the middle-income class party. Given the absence of a party representing their own interests, lower-income voters cannot be certain that the middle-income class party will honor its commitments. In other words, while the middle-income class party pledges to also champion the interests of the lower-income class before the election, the lower-income class cannot be sure that, post-election, the middle-income class will not impose taxes on the lower-income class and only redistribute wealth to the middle-income class. The lower-income class remains uncertain whether it will encounter a situation under the M-R model or under Director's law. Thus, the lower-income class evaluates whether backing the middle-income class will yield them greater disposable income through redistribution, or whether supporting the higher-income class will result in more disposable income due to a lower tax rate. In the second scenario, income redistribution cannot be anticipated even in the face of rising income inequality.

Let's denote λ as the probability that the middle-income class party will uphold its post-election promises. Given that λ lies between the values of 0 and $\lambda \leq 1$, the closer λ is to 1, the greater the likelihood that the middle-class party will keep its promises. In this case, the decision of the lower-income class about whom to vote for is determined by the following equation.

$$\lambda\left[a_l\left(1-t_{mr}\right)+n_2 g-\frac{cg^2}{2}n_2\right]+\left(1-\lambda\right)\left[a_l\left(1-t_{dr}\right)\right]<a_l\left(1-t_{pr}\right) \quad (4.12)$$

The left-hand side of Equation 4.12 represents the expected disposable income when the lower-income class votes for the middle-income class party, based on trust (λ). Conversely, the right-hand side represents the expected disposable income that the lower-income class will receive if they vote for the higher-income class party. The first element of the left-hand side of the equation represents a scenario where the M-R's case applies as a result of the middle-income class party keeping the promises it made before the election. The second element represents a scenario where the middle-income class does not keep its promises, and Director's law applies. Thus, the left-hand side uses trust as the basis for a weighted evaluation of the predicted disposable income of the lower-income class. On the right-hand side of the equation, because the lower-income voters voluntarily decide to vote for the higher-income class party based on expected disposable income, income redistribution occurs only in favor of the higher-income class.[8]

As seen in Equation 4.13, derived from Equation 4.12, when the level of trust (λ) drops below a certain level (λ^*), the lower-income voters cast their vote for the higher-income class party and wealth redistribution does not take place.[9]

$$\lambda<\lambda^*=\frac{a_l\left(1-t_{pr}\right)}{a_l\left(t_{dr}-t_{mr}\right)+n_2 t_{mr}-\frac{ct_{mr}^2}{2}n_2} \quad (4.13)$$

The following transpires when $\lambda < \lambda^*$.

$$y_h = (1-t)a_h + g - \frac{cg^2}{2} \tag{4.6}$$

$$y_m = a_m(1-t) \tag{3.7}$$

$$y_l = a_l(1-t) \tag{3.8}$$

When no party voices the interests of the lower-income class and trust in the middle-class party is low among this group, the tax rate aligns with the tax rate (t_{pr}) under a policy regime:

$$t_{pr} = \frac{1-a_h}{c} \tag{4.7}$$

Case 5: Class betrayal voting due to identity cleavages

Contrary to the M-R model, we assume that a society harbors not only economic cleavages but also identity cleavages. Therefore, unlike the scenarios described above, each class will prefer different types of in-kind transfers. In this instance, the middle-income class does not hold an absolute majority. For either the middle-income class party or the higher-income class party to secure election victory, they must garner the support of the lower-income class (Equation 4.11). Furthermore, identity significantly influences the lower-income class's choice of ally. The lower-income class weighs not only economic interests but also identity when selecting a coalition partner. By backing the class that represents an identity more akin to its own, the lower-income class seeks to minimize its losses (Waldfogel-type loss) and maximize its disposable income (Waldfogel, 2001).

Unlike previous scenarios, we now assume that redistribution benefits all classes. However, as the types of in-kind transfers are chosen by the coalition-forming classes, the class left out of the coalition does not receive its preferred type of redistribution, likely suffering relatively high losses from that redistribution (or high γ_i).

We can explore the following two sub-cases.

In the first case (Case 5-1), the interests of the lower-income class align closely with those of the middle-income class in terms of income redistribution. However, the lower- and higher-income voters share a similar identity (religion, race, ethnicity, etc.), leading the lower-income class to support the higher-income class by forming a coalition. In this scenario, the tax rate is set at a level that maximizes the sum of the disposable incomes of the coalition-forming lower- and higher-income voters. The types of in-kind transfers provided are those preferred by both the lower- and higher-income classes.

The second case (Case 5-2) assumes that the lower- and middle-income classes share similar redistribution interests and identity, thus forming a coalition. Under this scenario, redistribution is implemented based on the types of in-kind transfers favored jointly by the lower- and middle-income classes. The tax rate is set at a level that maximizes the sum of the coalition's disposable income.

Case 5-1: Coalition between the lower- and higher-income classes

$$y_h = a_h(1-t)+(1-\gamma_{hl})\left(n_h g - \frac{cg^2}{2}n_h\right) \tag{4.14}$$

$$y_m = a_m(1-t)+(1-\gamma_m)\left(n_m g - \frac{cg^2}{2}n_m\right) \tag{4.15}$$

$$y_l = a_l(1-t)+(1-\gamma_{hl})\left(n_l g - \frac{cg^2}{2}n_l\right) \tag{4.16}$$

where $\gamma_m > \gamma_{hl}$.

As the lower- and higher-income classes share similar identities, the lower-income class supports the higher-income class party. Taxes are paid by all classes, but the types of in-kind transfers chosen are favorable to both the lower-income and higher-income classes (Equations 4.14 and 4.16). γ_{hl} denotes the parameter of mismatch between the types of in-kind transfers that are actually provided and the respective types preferred by the coalition-forming lower- and higher-income classes. Thus, γ_{hl} reflects the level of similarity between the identities of the lower- and higher-income classes.[10] The closer γ_{hl} is to 0, the closer the similarities between their identities. γ_m represents the loss incurred by the middle-income class excluded from the coalition ($\gamma_m > \gamma_{hl}$). The chosen tax rate maximizes the sum of the disposable incomes of those in the governing coalition (lower-income class income + higher-income class income).

We substitute the balanced budget constraint formula ($g = t$) into equation 4.14.

$$y_h = a_h(1-t)+(1-\gamma_{hl})\left(n_h t - \frac{ct^2}{2}n_h\right) \tag{4.17}$$

We substitute $g = t$ into Equation 4.16.

$$y_l = a_l(1-t)+(1-\gamma_{hl})\left(n_l t - \frac{ct^2}{2}n_l\right) \tag{4.18}$$

The sum of the disposable incomes of the lower- and higher-income classes (y_{hl}^{c}), or the addition of Equations 4.17 and 4.18, is represented by Equation 4.19.

$$y_{hl}^{c} = (a_h + a_l) - t(a_h + a_l) + (1 - \gamma_{hl})(n_h + n_l)\left(t - c\frac{t^2}{2}\right) \tag{4.19}$$

Then the tax rate (t_{hl}) that maximizes y_{hl}^{c} can be written as follows.

$$t_{hl} = \frac{a_m - n_m - \gamma_{hl} + n_m \gamma_{hl}}{c(1 - \gamma_{hl})(1 - n_m)} \tag{4.20}$$

Since tax rate t_{hl} is positive, we assume $a_m > n_m(1 - \gamma_{hl}) + \gamma_{hl} = a_m^*$.

Figure 4.6 illustrates that as the market income of the middle-income class increases, so does the tax rate, enabling more wealth to be redistributed to the lower- and higher-income classes. This contrasts with the situation under Director's law, where the middle-income class sacrifices to maximize the wealth of the lower- and higher-income classes, rather than the lower- and higher-income classes sacrificing for the middle-income class. The rise to power of Silvio Berlusconi, an Italian politician and tycoon, as the leader of a political coalition between the lower- and higher-income classes following the global financial crisis, serves as a prime example of this case (Amable and Palombarini, 2014).

Case 5-2: Coalition between lower- and middle-income classes

A coalition is formed by the lower- and middle-income classes. All classes pay taxes, but the types of in-kind transfers are selected to favor both the lower- and middle-income classes (Equations 4.22 and 4.23). Tax rates are set at a level that maximizes the combined disposable income of the middle- and lower-income classes. γ_{ml} denotes the parameter of mismatch between the types of in-kind transfers actually transferred and the types preferred by the lower- and middle-income classes forming the coalition. Thus, γ_{ml} reflects the degree of similarity between the identities of the lower- and middle-income classes. γ_h represents the loss incurred when the higher-income class does not receive the types of in-kind transfers it prefers ($\gamma_h > \gamma_{ml}$).

$$y_h = a_h(1 - t) + (1 - \gamma_h)\left(n_h g - \frac{cg^2}{2} n_h\right) \tag{4.21}$$

$$y_m = a_m(1 - t) + (1 - \gamma_{ml})\left(n_m g - \frac{cg^2}{2} n_m\right) \tag{4.22}$$

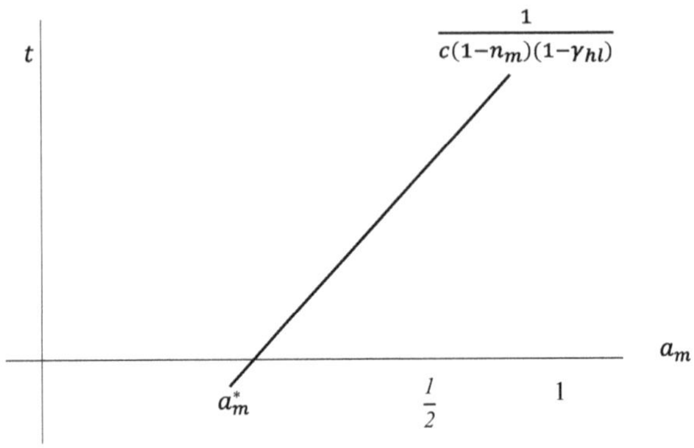

Figure 4.6 Coalition between lower- and higher-income classes

$$y_l = a_l(1-t)+(1-\gamma_{ml})\left(n_l g - \frac{cg^2}{2} n_l\right) \tag{4.23}$$

We substitute $g = t$ into Equation (4.22).

$$y_m = a_m(1-t)+(1-\gamma_{ml})\left(n_m t - \frac{ct^2}{2} n_m\right) \tag{4.24}$$

We also substitute $g = t$ into Equation (4.23).

$$y_l = a_l(1-t)+(1-\gamma_{ml})\left(n_l t - \frac{ct^2}{2} n_l\right) \tag{4.25}$$

Adding together the disposable income of the middle- and lower-income classes (y^c_{ml}) —that is, the sum of Equations 4.24 and 4.25—yields Equation 4.26.)

$$y^c_{hl} = (a_m + a_l) - t(a_m + a_l) + (1-\gamma_{ml})(n_m + n_l)\left(t - c\frac{t^2}{2}\right) \tag{4.26}$$

The tax rate (t_{ml}) that maximizes y^c_{ml} can thus be derived as follows.

$$t_{ml} = \frac{a_h - n_h - \gamma_{ml} + n_h\gamma_{ml}}{c(1-\gamma_{ml})(1-n_h)} \tag{4.27}$$

Since the tax rate (t_{hl}) is positive, we assume $a_h > n_h(1-\gamma_{ml}) + \gamma_{ml} = a^*_h$.

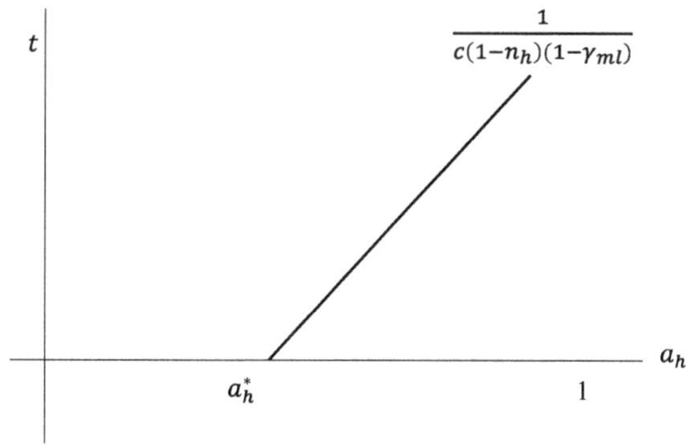

Figure 4.7 Coalition between the lower- and middle-income classes

As depicted in Figure 4.7, when the lower- and middle-income classes form a coalition, the larger the income inequality or economic cleavage, the higher the tax rate and redistribution to the lower- and middle-income classes.

The lower-income class determines its coalition partner by comparing the outcomes under Equations 4.16 and 4.23).

$$\gamma_{hl} < \gamma_{hl}^{*} = \frac{2}{t_{hl}\left(2 - ct_{hl}\right)}\left[\frac{a_l}{n_l}\left(t_{ml} - t_{hl}\right) + \left(t_{hl} - t_{ml}\right) - \frac{c}{2}\left(t_{hl}^2 - t_{ml}^2\right) + \gamma_{ml}\left(t_{ml} - \frac{ct_{ml}^2}{2}\right)\right] \quad (4.28)$$

As shown in Equation 4.28, when the identities of the lower- and higher-income classes are sufficiently similar (or $\gamma_{hl} < \gamma_{hl}^{*}$), the lower-income class can maximize its disposable income by forming a coalition with the higher-income class and minimizing losses.

Recent studies of populism in the US and Europe highlight politicians who emphasize issues related more to identity cleavages (e.g., racial, tribal, religious, ideological, regional) than economic cleavages. Populist parties fragment the lower- and middle-income classes by downplaying the significance of redistribution, instead highlighting issues such as tribal conflict, racial conflict, abortion, regional conflict, ideological debate, and religious conflict. If the party representing the higher-income class can successfully elevate these topics to prominence, the lower-income class is more likely to vote for the higher-income class party, resulting in class betrayal voting, which occurs when identity cleavages overshadow economic cleavages.

A notable instance of class betrayal voting is the welfare system reform in the US during the 1980s. The Republican party depicted the reform as a conflict between blacks and other people of color (portrayed as welfare recipients not working) and white laborers (portrayed as hardworking taxpayers). By framing the vote in this manner, the higher-income class managed to persuade lower-income class white, working voters to also vote for higher-income class interests, leading to a significant number of class betrayal votes. Moreover, in Kansas, a state with a low average income but a high number of Christian families, politicians persuaded Kansan voters that the election was about abortion and sexual minorities, leading voters to support the Republican party, which represents the interests of the higher-income class (Frank, 2004).

4.2.2 *Results of income redistribution*

We examined a total of nine different political regimes, including the M-R's model, and compared market income inequality with disposable income inequality under each scenario to directly measure the effectiveness of the respective income redistribution policies. Market income inequality was gauged by the difference ($a_h - (a_l + a_m)$) between the market income of the higher-income class (a_h) and the combined market incomes of the middle- and lower-income classes ($a_l + a_m$). Disposable income inequality was gauged by the difference ($y_h - (y_l + y_m)$) between the disposable income of the higher-income class (y_h) and the combined disposable incomes of the middle- and lower-income classes. Thus, the following case would represent an outcome of income inequality mitigation:

$$y_h - (y_l + y_m) < a_h - (a_l + a_m) \quad (4.29)$$

In Table 4.1, we have summarized our analysis of each of the nine political regimes and indicated whether income inequality is alleviated or not under the respective regime.

As anticipated, redistribution policies under an autocracy exacerbate income inequality, while in the Director's law and M-R's model scenarios, taxation and redistribution reduce income inequality. However, in a captured democracy, if β is small enough to satisfy $\beta < \beta^* = \left(1 - \frac{ct_c}{2} - a_h + a_m + a_l\right)$, then, unlike the M-R's model, taxation and redistribution could exacerbate income inequality. Similarly, a policy regime ($\beta = 0$) could result in worsening income inequality after taxation and distribution. Under high levels of government corruption, significant losses occur as a result of redistribution, especially compared to the M-R's model, but income inequality is reduced if net transfers in-kind by government ($\widehat{g}_i$) are positive. However, compared with M-R, if the level of corruption surpasses a certain threshold $\left(c' > c^* = \frac{2}{t_{tr}^2}\left[(1 + a_h - a_m - a_l)(t_{tr} - t_{mr}) + \frac{ct_{mr}^2}{2}\right]\right)$, the loss becomes large enough to cause net redistribution to decrease. Next, when analyzing the scenario where no party represents the interests of the lower-income class, we observe that, similar to the policy regime case, if the lower-income class's level of trust in the middle-income class party is low enough ($\lambda < \lambda^*$), post-redistribution income inequality is exacerbated, not mitigated.

Table 4.1 Comparison of market income inequality and disposable income inequality under different political regimes

Political regime	*Comparison of market income inequality and disposable income inequality*
Autocracy	Because $y_h - (y_m + y_l) > a_h - (a_m + a_l)$, redistribution $(y_h - (y_m + y_l))$ further aggravates income inequality, making post-distribution inequality higher than pre-distribution inequality $(a_h - (a_m + a_l))$. $$\left(y_h-\left(y_m+y_l\right)\right)-\left(a_h-\left(a_m+a_l\right)\right)=t_a-c\frac{t_a^2}{2}+t_a\left(1-a_h\right)>0$$
Director's law	Because $y_h - (y_m + y_l) < a_h - (a_m + a_l)$, income inequality improves under this scenario, making post-distribution inequality lower than pre-distribution inequality. $$\left(y_h-\left(y_m+y_l\right)\right)-\left(a_h-\left(a_m+a_l\right)\right)=-t_{dr}\left(a_h-a_m-a_l\right)-t_{dr}+c\frac{t_{dr}^2}{2}<0$$
M-R's model	Because $y_h - (y_m + y_l) < a_h - (a_m + a_l)$, income inequality improves under this scenario, making post-distribution inequality lower than pre-distribution inequality. $(y_h - (y_m + y_l)) - (a_h - (a_m + a_l))=$ $$-t_{mr}\left(a_h-a_m-a_l\right)-n_l t_{mr}+c\frac{t_{mr}^2}{2}n_1-n_2 t_{mr}+c\frac{t_{mr}^2}{2}n_2<0$$
Captured democracy	If the cost to gain de facto political power is low enough $\left(\beta<\beta^*=\left(1-\frac{ct_c}{2}-a_h+a_m+a_l\right)\right)$, then, because $y_h - (y_m + y_l) > a_h - (a_m + a_l)$, policy implementation further aggravates income inequality, making post-distribution inequality higher than pre-distribution inequality. $$\left(y_h-\left(y_m+y_l\right)\right)-\left(a_h-\left(a_m+a_l\right)\right)=-t_c\left(a_h-a_m-a_l\right)+\left(1-\beta\right)t_c+c\frac{t_c^2}{2}>0$$
Policy regime (higher-income class-friendly policy regime)	Because $y_h - (y_m + y_l) > a_h - (a_m + a_l)$, policy implementation further aggravates income inequality, making post-distribution inequality higher than pre-distribution inequality. For $\left(y_h-\left(y_m+y_l\right)\right)$ $-\left(a_h-\left(a_m+a_l\right)\right)=-t_{pr}\left(a_h-a_m-a_l\right)+t_{pr}-c\frac{t_{pr}^2}{2}$ to be true, $\frac{4\left(1-a_h\right)}{c}$ must be $> t_{pr}$. However, because $t_{pr}=\frac{1-a_h}{c}$ and $\frac{4\left(1-a_h\right)}{c}>t_{pr}$, $y_h - (y_m + y_l) > a_h - (a_m + a_l)$.

(*Continued*)

Table 4.1 (Continued)

Political regime	*Comparison of market income inequality and disposable income inequality*
Corrupt government	Even if corruption leads to large losses, if net transfers in-kind are positive (+), or if $n_1 g - \frac{c' g^2}{2} n_1 > 0$ and $n_2 g - \frac{c' g^2}{2} n_2 > 0$, then $y_h - (y_m + y_l) - (a_h - (a_m + a_l)) = -t_{mr}(a_h - a_m - a_l) - n_1 t_{mr} + c' \frac{t_{mr}^2}{2} n_1 - n_2 t_{mr} + c' \frac{t_{mr}^2}{2} n_2 < 0$. Because $y_h - (y_m + y_l) < a_h - (a_m + a_l)$, income inequality improves under this scenario, making post-distribution inequality lower than pre-distribution inequality. However, if $c' > c^* = \frac{2}{t_{tr}^2}[(1 + a_h - a_m - a_l)(t_{tr} - t_{mr}) + \frac{c t_{mr}^2}{2}$ (i.e., if government corruption surpasses a certain level, thus creating large leakages in the processes of redistribution), then redistribution may be less effective than under the M-R's model.
Absence of a party representing the interests of the lower-income class	If the lower-income class's trust in the party of the middle-income class is sufficiently low ($\lambda < \lambda^*$), the outcomes from the absence of a party for the lower-income class resemble those under a policy regime. This is because $y_h - (y_m + y_l) > a_h - (a_m + a_l)$, policy implementation exacerbates income inequality, resulting in post-distribution inequality being higher than pre-distribution inequality.
Identity cleavage: coalition between lower-income class and higher-income class (class betrayal vote)	If $\gamma_m > \frac{2}{t_{hl} n_m (2 - c t_{hl})}\left[\left(n_m t_{hl} - c\frac{t_{hl}^2}{2} n_m\right) + \left(n_l t_{hl} - c\frac{t_{hl}^2}{2} n_l\right)(1 - \gamma_{hl}) - \left(n_h t_{hl} - c\frac{t_{hl}^2}{2} n_h\right)(1 - \gamma_{hl}) + t_{hl}(a_h - a_m - a_l)\right]$ (i.e., if the identity of the middle-income class markedly differs from that of the lower- and higher-income classes), then, because $y_h - (y_m + y_l) > a_h - (a_m + a_l)$, policy implementation exacerbates income inequality, leading to post-distribution inequality being higher than pre-distribution inequality.
Identity cleavage: coalition between lower-income class and middle-income class	If $\gamma_{ml} < \frac{2}{(n_m + n_l) t_{ml} (2 - c t_{ml})}\left[\left(n_l t_{ml} - c\frac{t_{ml}^2}{2} n_l\right) + \left(n_m t_{ml} - c\frac{t_{ml}^2}{2} n_m\right) - \left(n_h t_{ml} - c\frac{t_{ml}^2}{2} n_h\right)(1 - \gamma_h) + t_{ml}(a_h - a_m - a_l)\right]$, (i.e., if the identities of the middle- and lower-income classes are sufficiently similar), then, because $y_h - (y_m + y_l) < a_h - (a_m + a_l)$, income inequality improves under this scenario, resulting in post-distribution inequality being lower than pre-distribution inequality.

Lastly, we examined two scenarios with identity cleavages. If the lower- and higher-income classes exhibit very similar identities that are also different from those of the middle-income class, then income inequality will be exacerbated through redistribution. This corresponds to class betrayal voting, where the higher-income class emphasizes race, religion, and other social issues to divide the weakly bonded middle- and lower-income classes. Conversely, if the middle- and lower-income classes share a similar identity, redistribution can lead to an alleviation of income inequality. Studying the nine different cases, we observe that, unlike the prediction made by M-R, democracy does not always lead to income redistribution that improves income inequality. For instance, when the higher-income class wields *de facto* political power, when a higher-income class-friendly policy regime exists, when government corruption is extremely high, when no party represents the interests of the lower-income class, or when the lower- and higher-income classes share a similar identity, redistribution policies can be ineffective, and even aggravate income inequality.

4.3 Conclusion

This chapter discusses income inequality, a topic currently attracting significant attention from researchers and politicians, within the context of the interaction between the economic and political domains. M-R posited that under democracy, policies promoting income redistribution would be enacted, alleviating income inequality and safeguarding the economic interests of lower- and middle-income voters. They further argued that since democracy extends suffrage to a larger populace, irrespective of income level, if a political mechanism exists to coordinate the interests of lower- and middle-income voters, government can ameliorate income inequality through redistribution policies. If M-R's theory were applicable in practice, the global proliferation of democracy should have mitigated income inequality worldwide. However, contrary to the theory's expectations, nearly all countries have witnessed a rise in income inequality. Subsequent studies into M-R's model have unequivocally demonstrated that the relationships between democracy, redistribution, and inequality are not as straightforward as the model proposes.

We draw on previous political and economic research to model why income inequality has escalated in many countries over the past four decades despite the implementation of redistribution policies, and why such policies often lacked efficacy. We conclude that when the higher-income class exercises *de facto* political power, when a policy regime favorable to the higher-income class exists, when government corruption is exceedingly high, when no party represents the interests of the lower-income class, or when the lower- and higher-income classes share a similar identity, redistribution policies can be ineffective, and even exacerbate income inequality.

As Acemoglu and Robinson (2012 and 2015) elucidate, economists often presume complex political problems have been fully understood or focus only on political problems that have been resolved. Consequently, economists sometimes harbor naive beliefs that identifying appropriate economic solutions is the key to effortlessly resolving social issues. However, as our study illustrates, researchers need to concentrate on the interactions between chosen policy and the power distribution among socio-political groups, and how these institutions, policies, and laws influence the bargaining power and *de facto* power of each group (Boyer, 2015).

Appendix

Piketty's explanation for the enduring income inequality framed within the context of the cleavage theory

In 2014, Thomas Piketty's book *Capital in the Twenty-First Century* made a significant impact, being published in English, translated into 30 languages, and selling 2.2 million copies worldwide. The book garnered widespread interest and support due to Piketty's insightful analysis and proposed solutions for tackling income inequality. However, despite this public interest and support, the issue of income inequality did not experience substantial improvement even after the book's release. Piketty's recommended policies to address income inequality, including progressive income tax and a global capital tax, have yet to be put into practice. In 2022, Piketty himself offered an explanation for this situation. He conducted an empirical analysis of three countries—Britain, the United States, and France—using post-election survey data spanning from 1948 to 2020 (Gethin et al., 2022). Piketty's research revealed that as globalization advanced, the traditional left-wing advocates for income redistribution were joined by a group of highly educated experts who favored globalization. This division within the left-wing camp resulted in a split among those advocating for income redistribution: On one side, there were the highly educated experts who embraced globalization and its economic policies, and on the other side, there were the low-educated and low-skilled groups who opposed globalization (refer to Figure A-4.1). Currently, countries are witnessing shifts in their alliances. Both the United States and France are undergoing a realignment, with a globalist alliance forming, composed of highly educated, high-income, and wealthy individuals, while an opposing anti-globalist alliance is emerging, consisting of low-educated, low-income, and self-employed individuals. Additionally, the UK is experiencing a realignment, leading to a division between the elite and the high-income and wealthy elite.

This cleavage within the left-wing camp created a barrier to the adoption of income redistribution policies, despite the ongoing increase in income inequality. The inability to form a united coalition in support of income redistribution has made it difficult to implement effective policies to address income inequality. Consequently, the adoption of redistribution policies remains a challenging task at present. In conclusion, although Piketty's analysis and proposed solutions for income inequality gained global attention and support, the

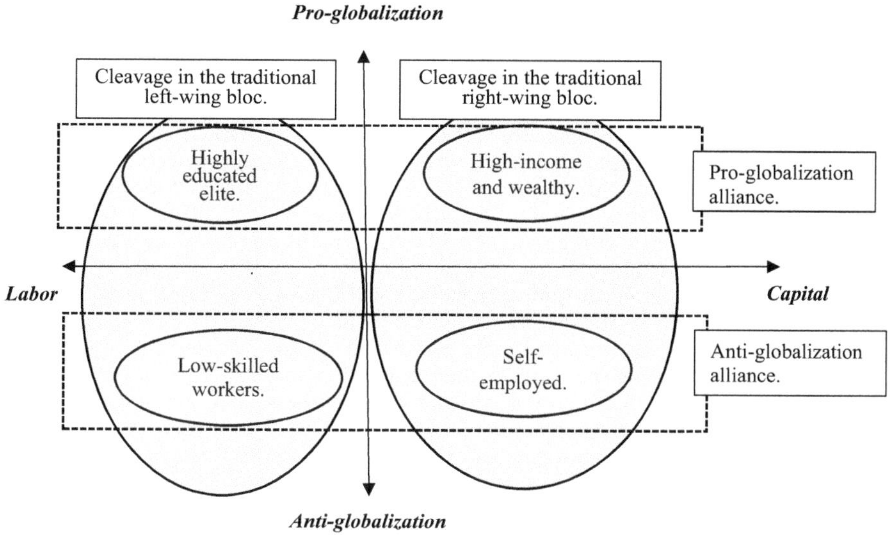

Figure A-4.1 Piketty's explanation for the rise of income inequality since the 1980s is based on a new cleavage

actual implementation of his policies has been hindered by a division within the left-wing camp, resulting from the impact of globalization on varying economic interests and perspectives. Until a new coalition can bridge this gap and rally support for income redistribution, meaningful policies to address income inequality will continue to face difficulties in being realized.

Piketty's research emphasizes the significance of analyzing the *political process*, with a particular focus on the *distribution of power*, to gain insight into how new policies are formulated and adopted. According to Piketty, the success of policy adoption is not solely contingent on the quality of its content but also relies on building strong political alliances. In other words, even if a policy is grounded in sound economic principles and targets specific objectives, its effective implementation hinges on garnering support from influential political actors. Consequently, while a policy is crafted as an economic process aimed at achieving specific outcomes through the establishment of new macroscopic relationships between variables, its actual formation and adoption are inherently political processes shaped by power dynamics. This highlights the necessity of adopting a political economy perspective that delves into the intricate interplay between economic forces and political actors to comprehensively understand policy dynamics.

In essence, Piketty's research underscores the importance of considering both economic and political factors when analyzing the inception, acceptance, and execution of policies. Gaining an understanding of power distribution and the involvement of key political allies becomes crucial in determining the fate of proposed policies, regardless of their economic soundness.

Notes

1 Beyond elections, a marked contrast in political participation is particularly evident in campaign contributions. The affluent segment displays a striking 56% participation rate in donating to campaigns, while the low-income group contributes a mere 6%. In 2012, the top 0.01% income bracket in the United States accounted for 40% of all campaign contributions. Moreover, significant disparities were observed in political engagement with organizations, with three-quarters of the wealthy class actively involved in various political activities, while only 13% of the impoverished class participated. According to a report by the American Political Science Association (2004), the lack of political representation for the middle and lower class was identified as another contributing factor to the widening of political inequality.

2 Refer to the Appendix for Piketty's argument, which explains the persistence of income inequality in developed economies through the lens of the cleavage theory.

3 Policy regime signifies the fundamental foundation and structure of government policies aimed at economic management. It encompasses the guiding principles, ideologies, the theoretical and systematic formulation of these policies, the instruments used to implement them, and the political and social implications arising from their implementation. Przeworski (2014) differentiates various policy regimes based on principles related to ownership, unemployment strategies, welfare programs, and international agreements.

4 According to Bresser-Pereira, several factors shape the formation of a new policy regime. Firstly, the presence of intellectuals who represent the interests of specific social classes and offer new alternatives for crisis escape is crucial. Thinkers such as Friedman, Hayek, and Popper played a pivotal role in establishing the foundation of the neoliberal policy regime by introducing novel principles and policy tools. Additionally, effective political leadership is essential to guide the formation of political alliances centered around these innovative ideas and policy alternatives. Moreover, efficient mechanisms should be in place to assess and communicate the soundness and legitimacy of a particular policy alternative to citizens amidst competing options. Lastly, as observed in East Asia and South America, the pressure from international organizations during times of crisis also significantly contributes to the emergence of a new policy regime.

5 Iversen and Soskice's (2009) model, focusing on cross-national comparative analysis during the same period, encounters challenges when explaining changes over time within a single country. For instance, it struggles to account for why income inequality worsens, welfare expenditures decrease, and government spending decreases in a specific country, despite maintaining the same electoral system. Consider the United States: during the New Deal era, it witnessed the emergence of a historically egalitarian society with pro-labor and pro-welfare policies. However, after the rise of neoliberal policies in the 1980s, income distribution deteriorated. Despite the United States retaining a majoritarian political framework, what explains such temporal variations? Furthermore, explaining the diversity between countries with the same electoral system, such as the differences in redistributive and welfare spending among Nordic countries, Italy, Greece, Spain, and Portugal under proportional representation, presents a challenge. Iversen and Soskice (2009) shed some light on these questions. During the Fordist era, a complementary relationship existed between skilled and unskilled labor in the production process, enabling collective bargaining for solidarity wages and employment stability. Additionally, as unskilled workers represented the median voter, majoritarian two-party systems also catered to their preferences, resulting in income redistribution and welfare program adoption. However, with the advent of liberalization, globalization, and the rise of knowledge economies, collective bargaining transitioned to individual bargaining, disrupting the symbiotic relationship between skilled and

unskilled labor. This shift led to the decline of solidarity wages and weakened job protection for unskilled labor, reclassifying them into the low-skilled labor category and expanding the wage gap between skilled and unskilled workers. In the post-Fordist era, unskilled laborers gradually lost their relevance as median voters and were excluded from policy considerations, resulting in a retreat from income redistribution policies aimed at them. Conversely, under a proportional representation system, if a center-left coalition forms, incorporating unskilled laborers, redistributive policies and proactive labor market policies for this group might be implemented. However, in countries with strong centrist parties based on non-class cleavages, like Germany's Christian Democratic Union, fractures appear around religious lines, prompting some left-leaning voters to shift to centrist parties, thereby weakening support for left-wing parties. As a result, left-leaning coalitions diminish, making it difficult to adopt social policies for unskilled or low-skilled laborers. Iversen and Soskice's primary explanations center around the weakening of collective bargaining, which helps elucidate the differences between the Fordist and post-Fordist eras. They also illuminate variations in social policies among countries under the proportional representation system by focusing on the potential and content of political coalitions.

6 While Iversen and Soskice emphasize the role of political institutions in political coalition formation, Blyth (2002) and Rodrik (2014) underscore the role of ideas, and Amable and Palombarini (2014) highlight the leadership of politicians (the ability of politicians to form coalitions through policy mediation).
7 Iversen and Soskice's (2009) model presumes the existence of only right- and left-wing parties, with no party representing the middle-income class.
8 We assume a tax rate (t_{pr}) equal to that under a policy regime, where the higher-income class does not need to incur additional costs to set a tax rate most advantageous to themselves.
9 We posit the existence of balanced budget constraints.
10 We assume that the identity gap is based on a reference point equidistant from the identity of both classes.

References

Acemoglu, D. and J. A. Robinson (2015), "The rise and decline of general laws of capitalism," *Journal of Economic Perspectives*, Vol. 29, No. 1, pp. 3–28.

Acemoglu, D. and J. Robinson (2012), *Why nations fail: The origins of power, prosperity, and poverty*, New York: Crown Business.

Acemoglu, D., S. Naidu, P. Restrepo, and J. A. Robinson (2013), "Democracy, redistribution and inequality," *NBER Working Paper*, No. 19746.

Amable, B. and S. Palombarini (2014), "The bloc bourgeois in France and Italy," in Magara, E. (ed), *Economic crises and policy regimes*, Cheltenham: Edward Elgar Publishing Limited.

American Political Science Association Task Force (2004), "American democracy in an age of rising inequality," *Perspectives on Politics*, Vol. 2, No. 4, pp. 651–666.

Bartel, L. (2008), *Unequal democracy: The political economy of a new gilded age*, Princeton, NJ: Princeton University.

Bénabou, R. and E. A. Ok (2001), "Social mobility and the demand for redistribution: The POUM hypothesis," *Quarterly Journal of Economics*, Vol. 116, No. 2, pp. 447–487.

Blyth, M. (2002), *Great transformations*, New York: Cambridge University Press.

Boyer, R. (2015), *Économie politique des capitalisms*, Paris: La Découverte.

Boyer, R. (2014), "How do polity and economy interact within Regulation Theory? Consequences for policy regimes and reform strategies," pp. 124–173, Cheltenham: Edward Elgar Publishing Limited.

Bresser-Pereira, L. C. (2014), "The hegemony constraints in the neoliberal years of capitalism," in Magara, E. (ed), *Economic crises and policy regimes*, pp. 56–78, Cheltenham: Edward Elgar Publishing Limited.
Choi, J. (2010), *Democracy after democratization*, Seoul: Humanitas.
Cruces, G., R. Perez-Truglia, and M. Tetaz (2013), "Biased perception of income distribution and preferences for redistribution: Evidence from a survey experiment," *Journal of Public Economics*, Vol. 98, pp. 100–112.
Downs, A. (1957), *An economic theory of democracy*, New York: Harper and Row Publishers.
Frank, T. (2004): *What's the matter with Kansas?* New York: Henry Holt and Company.
Gethin, A., C. Martínez-Toledano, and T. Piketty (2022), "Brahmin left versus merchant right: Changing political cleavages in 21 western democracies, 1948–2020," *The Quarterly Journal of Economics*, Vol. 137, No. 1, pp. 1–48.
Gradstein, M. and B. Milanovic (2004), "Does liberté = egalité? A survey of the empirical links between democracy and inequality with some evidence on the transition economies," *Journal of Economic Surveys*, Vol. 18, No. 4, pp.515–537.
Hacker, J. and P. Pierson (2010), *Winner-take-all politics: How Washington made the rich richer and turned its back on the middle Class*, New York: Simon & Schuster Paperbacks.
Hall, P. A. and D. Soskice (2001), *Varieties of capitalism: The institutional foundations of comparative advantage*, Oxford: Oxford University Press.
Hetherington, M. J. (2004), *Why Trust Matters: Declining political trust and the demise of American liberalism*, Princeton, NJ: Princeton University Press.
Iversen, T. and D. Soskice (2009), "Distribution and redistribution: The shadow of the nineteenth century," *World Politics*, Vol. 61, No. 3, pp. 438–486.
Lijphart, A. (2012), *Patterns of democracy: Government forms and performance in thirty-six countries*, New Haven: Yale University Press.
Lipset, S. M. and S. Rokkan (1967), "Cleavage structures, party systems and voter alignments: An introduction," in Lipset, S. M. and S. Rokkan (eds.), *Party systems and voter alignments: Cross-national perspectives*, New York: Free Press.
Marshall, M. G. and T. R. Gurr (2020), *Polity V project, political regime characteristics and transitions, 1800–2018*, Vienna Center for Systemic Peace.
Marshall, M. G. and G. C. Elzinga-Marshall (2017), *Global report 2017: Conflict, governance and state fragility*, Vienna, VA: Center for Systemic Peace.
Meltzer, A. H. and S. F. Richard (1981), "A rational theory of the size of government," *Journal of Political Economy*, Vol. 89, No. 5, pp. 914–927.
Mulligan, C. B., R. Gil, and X. Sala-i-Martin (2004), "Do democracies have different public policies than non-democracies?" *Journal of Economic Perspectives*, Vol. 18, No. 1, pp. 51–74.
Piketty, T. (2014), *Capital in the twenty-first century*, Cambridge, MA: The Belknap Press of Harvard University Press.
Przeworski, A. (2014), "Choices and echoes: Stability and change of policy regimes," in Magara, E. (ed), *Economic crises and policy regimes*, pp 33–55, Cheltenham: Edward Elgar Publishing Limited.
Putnam, R. D. (1993), *Making democracy work: Civic tradition in modern Italy*, Princeton, NJ: Princeton University Press
Rodrik, D. (2014), "When ideas trump interests: Preferences, worldviews, and policy innovations," *Journal of Economic Perspectives*, Vol. 28, No. 1, pp. 189–208.
Romer, T. (1975), "Individual welfare, majority voting, and the properties of a linear income tax," *Journal of Public Economics*, Vol. 4, No. 2, pp. 163–185.
Rothstein, B. (2005), *Social traps and the problem of trust*, Cambridge: Cambridge University Press.
Schattschneider, E. E. (1960), *The semi-sovereign people: A realist view of democracy in America*, New York: Holt, Rinehart and Winston

Scheve, K. and Stasavage, D. (2012), "Democracy, war, and wealth: Lessons from two centuries of inheritance taxation," *American Political Science Review*, Vol. 106, No. 1, pp. 82–102.

Scheve, K. and Stasavage, D. (2010), "The conscription of wealth: Mass warfare and the demand for progressive taxation," *International Organization*, Vol. 64, No. 4, pp. 529–561.

Scheve, K. and Stasavage, D. (2009), "Institutions, partisanship, and inequality in the long run," *World Politics*, Vol. 61, No. 2, pp. 215–253.

Seon, H. (2015), *The dynamics of consensus democracy*, Gwangju: Chon Nam National University Press.

Sirowy, L. and A. Inkeles (1990), "The effects of democracy on economic growth and inequality: A review," *Studies in Comparative International Development*, Vol. 25, No. 1, pp. 126–157.

Stiglitz, J. E. (2012), *The price of inequality: How today's divided society endangers our future*, New York: W.W. Norton & Company.

Waldfogel, J. (2001), "The deadweight loss of Christmas," *American Economic Review*, Vol. 83, No. 5, pp. 1328–1336.

World Inequality Lab (2017), *World Inequality Report 2018*, http://wir2018.wid.world/

5 Estimation model specification and results

5.1 Estimation model specification

To examine the validity of the M-R hypothesis, this section as a first step employs the following baseline empirical model specification, considering redistribution, and assuming redistribution as a dependent variable. This approach aligns with related literature on the M-R hypothesis (Scervini, 2012; Ostry et al., 2014; Acemoglu et al., 2015; Seo and Kang, 2023).

$$ReD_{it} = \alpha_0 + \alpha_1 Gini_{it}^M + \alpha_2 Demo_{it} + X_{it}^{'}\alpha_3 + \mu_i + v_t + \varepsilon_{it} \quad (5.1)$$

ReD_{it} represents income redistribution, defined as the absolute difference between market income inequality and disposable income inequality in year t and country i. Market income refers to pre-tax and pre-transfer income, while disposable income is defined as income after tax imposition and various transfer incomes. Most income distribution comparison across countries in the related literature is conducted based on disposable income. This reflects the status of income inequality after government policies such as tax and transfers are implemented. However, redistribution (ReD) serves as a crucial indicator that identifies the government's role in income redistribution. Therefore, ReD values indicate the extent to which various tax and social welfare policies contribute to improving income distribution.

$Gini_{it}^M$ represents the status of market income Gini inequality, which reflects the status of income inequality before government redistribution policies are implemented. Therefore, it reflects the equity status of market mechanism in income distribution. $Demo_{it}$ reflects the degree of democratic status. X_{it}' is a vector of control variables. α_0, α_1, and α_2 are the parameters to be estimated, and α_3 is a set of parameters to be estimated. μ_i and v_t represent a set of country and year dummies, respectively, and ε_{it} denotes an error term for white noise.

The control variables considered in the empirical model specification above indicates the following implications.

First, $Gini_{it}^M$ aims to investigate the median voter hypothesis proposed by Meltzer and Richard (1981). This hypothesis posits that median voters are

DOI: 10.4324/9781032695754-5

more likely to support redistribution policies that reduce income inequality when the gap between pre-tax income and mean income increases. Therefore, the higher market income inequality with higher value of $Gini_{it}^{M}$ leads to higher redistribution with improvement of income distribution. Under the M-R hypothesis, the coefficient for $Gini_{it}^{M}$ is expected to be negative.

Second, *Demo* is to test the validity of the M-R hypothesis as well. Under the M-R hypothesis, the sign of the coefficient for $Demo_{it}$ is expected to be positive. According to the median voter hypothesis, a democratic system plays a positive role in improving income distribution, indicating a positive sign of the coefficient. To find robustness of various democratic indicators, three different democracy variables are estimated.

Third, X_{it}' represents a vector of economic variables considered to be main determinants, excluding market income inequality and democratic status. The variables are GDP per capita, GDP growth rate, and unemployment rate. These are derived from previous related literature on the studies of the M-R hypothesis (Milanovic, 2010; Scervini, 2012; Gründler and Köllner, 2017; Kammas and Sarantides, 2019). GDP per capita and GDP growth rate reflect the status and speed of economic development, while the unemployment rate is associated with the business cycle and various social redistribution and welfare policies such as unemployment benefits.[1]

In addition to testing the validity of the traditional M-R hypothesis, five main hypotheses are jointly tested with the following extended model specification.

$$ReD_{it} = \alpha_0 + \alpha_1 Gini_{it}^{M} + \alpha_2 Demo_{it}' + + X_{it}'\alpha_3 + \left(Gini_{it}^{M} \cdot Z_{it}'\right)\alpha_4 + \mu_i + v_t + \varepsilon_{it} \quad (5.2)$$

Z_{it}' is a vector of additional control variables that reflect the five hypotheses explained in Chapter 4, and α_4 is a vector of the parameters to be estimated. Other notations remain the same as in Equation 5.1. The extended model estimation aims to test the conditional validity of the M-R hypothesis. Or it can be interpreted that the estimation results examine why the M-R hypothesis does not hold.

The model can be estimated for both democratic and non-democratic countries, or separately. However, this study focuses on panel estimation for democratic countries since it is shown that there is not a strong relationship between redistribution and a democratic state for non-democratic countries. Further, the estimation results for the interaction term show the joint impact of market income distribution and five different hypotheses or effects of five hypotheses, assuming market income inequality is given. All other variables remain the same as in Equation 5.1.

Seo and Kang (2023) identify two distinct patterns between redistribution and market income inequality even among democratic countries but show that there is no significant relationship between redistribution and market income inequality for non-democratic countries. Therefore, this extended model specification aims to test why the M-R hypothesis does not hold even among democratic countries. For this purpose, only democratic countries are used for estimation by excluding non-democratic countries.

5.2 Data

The most crucial data for the empirical estimation is the income inequality indicator. The most commonly used inequality data are the World Income Inequality Database (WIID) (UNU-WIDER, 2022) and the Standardized World Income Inequality Database (SWIID). These two databases differ in the coverage of years and countries and data imputation for the missing years.

The WIID comprises real-income inequality data across countries and years but has many missing values. However, the SWIID database fills the missing values in the WIID database with data acquired through extensive data imputation (Solt, 2020). The SWIID, however, is criticized for the imputation itself as well as the method of imputation used (Ferreira et al., 2015; Jenkins, 2015). Despite this, many studies use the SWIID due to its extensive coverage of periods. This study utilizes the most recent updated version, SWIID 9_5. The data spans from 1965 to 2022, encompassing a varying number of countries by year. The maximum number of countries, 183, is reached in 2007, after which the number decreases over the years, with only 10 countries represented in 2022. Consequently, both datasets have their advantages and disadvantages for conducting empirical analysis.

Income redistribution (ReD) is defined as the difference between market income inequality and disposable income inequality. Figure 5.1 illustrates the trend of income redistribution for the period 1990–2021, excluding the 2022 data due to the small number of countries represented. The redistribution trend decreases until 2007, reflecting the diminishing impact of government redistribution policies. Post 2007, the trend reverses, indicating increasing redistribution values. However, caution is advised in interpretation as the pattern in Figure 5.1 does not derive from the balanced panel data of all countries.

Figure 5.2 depicts the relationship between redistribution and the Gini index as a market income inequality. This relationship is examined to validate the M-R hypothesis in a simple manner. Broadly speaking, a positive correlation exists between redistribution and market income inequality, affirming the M-R hypothesis. The simple regression of redistribution on market income inequality reveals a coefficient of 0.2130. However, two intriguing trends emerge. Firstly, there is a diverse variation of redistribution for the same level of market income inequality. We can identify very distinct trends over the same market income inequality. These trends can be divided into two groups: those below and those above the fitted line. For instance, countries below the fitted line can be interpreted as having less significant improvement in redistribution than the countries above the fitted line.

From Figures 5.1 to 5.2, it can be inferred that redistribution has improved but shows significant variation over the years. Therefore, it is necessary to find

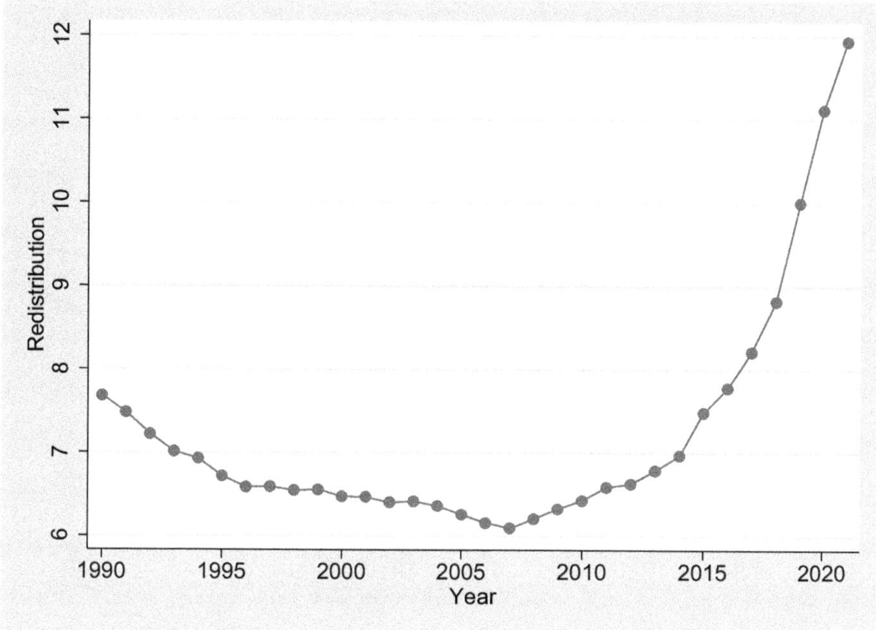

Figure 5.1 Income redistribution trends

Note: Redistribution is calculated as the difference between market and disposable income inequality.

certain factors that explain the variation of redistribution even for the same market income inequality. It is beyond the simple relationship between redistribution and market income inequality. In other words, market income inequality and/or democracy alone cannot be a sufficient factor to explain the change in redistribution.

Secondly, as another aspect of the M-R hypothesis, the impact of a democratic system on redistribution is examined. As we discussed above, Figures 5.1 and 5.2 suggest that market income inequality alone is insufficient to explain the degree of redistribution. Since the validity of the M-R hypothesis might yield different results with different measures of democratic state, this study employs three democracy measures that are used in related studies.[2]

The first indicator is the measures proposed by Boix et al. (2013, "BMR") during the 1800–2020 period for 222 distinct countries in the latest version 4.0. These values are recorded as dichotomous coding with 1 for democratic countries and 0 for non-democratic countries.

The second indicator is the measures proposed by Cheibub et al. (2010, "CGV") for the period 1946–2008 and 199 countries. This data is known as Democracy-Dictatorship (DD) or index of democracy and dictatorship and is also recorded as dummy indicators with 1 for democratic regimes and 0 for non-democratic countries.

Figure 5.2 Market income inequality and redistribution

Note: 1) Redistribution is calculated as the difference between market and disposable income inequality.
2) bhat is the estimation coefficient for the regression of redistribution on market income inequality.

The third democracy indicator is the Polity V, which covers the years 1800–2018. The dataset covers the 167 countries that are states with a total population of 500,000 or more in the most recent year. Unlike the previous two indicators, the Polity V scores are recorded as –10 to +10. It defines non-democratic countries with values from –10 to 5 and democratic countries with values from 6 to 10.[3] Non-democratic countries include autocracies (–10 to –6) and anocracies (–5 to +5 and –66, –77 and –88 of three special categories). To identify possible factors that explain the findings from Figures 5.1 and 5.2, Figure 5.3 tests the relation between redistribution and market income inequality by dividing the countries into democratic and non-democratic countries. The democracy indicator is derived from the BMR data. The top graph in Figure 5.3 represents the relation between redistribution and market income inequality for democratic countries only. Interestingly, two distinct country groups are clearly identified: one group with a very clear positive relation between redistribution and market income inequality, and another group with a less clear relation. However, the bottom graph in Figure 5.3 for non-democratic countries does not show a significant relation between redistribution and market income inequality.[4]

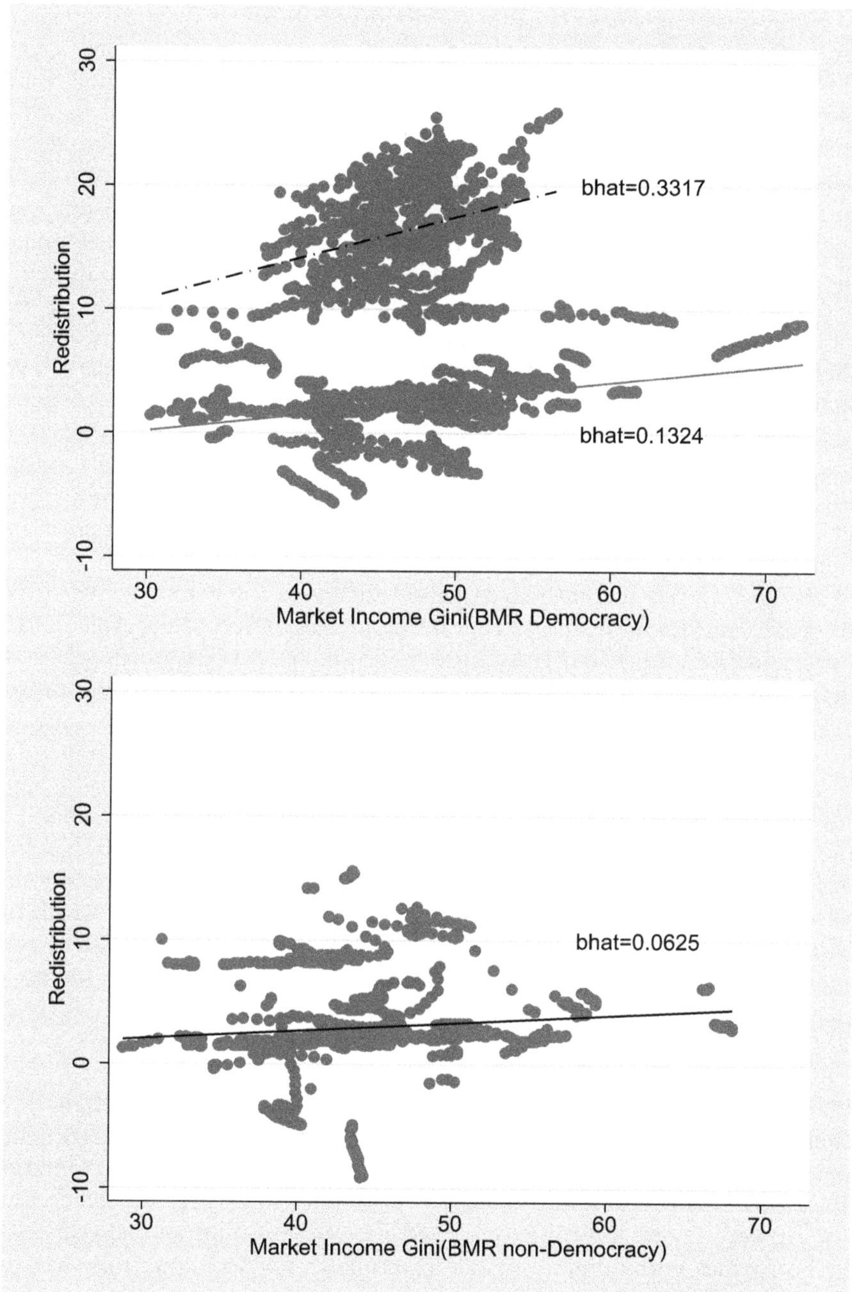

Figure 5.3 Market income inequality and redistribution by BMR democracy

Note: 1) Redistribution is calculated as the difference between market and disposable income inequality.
2) bhat is the estimation coefficient for the regression of redistribution on market income inequality.

Upon examining the implications of Figures 5.1–5.4, it becomes apparent that a more sophisticated econometric estimation is necessary to investigate the validity of the M-R hypothesis. Simply put, market income inequality and democratic status alone are insufficient to determine the validity of the M-R hypothesis. Hence, additional factors influencing redistribution should be considered as extensive literature review in Chapter 4 shows.

Thirdly, all economic indicators (GDP per capita, GDP growth rate, and unemployment rate) are sourced from the World Bank's World Development Indicators. GDP per capita is expressed in constant 2015 USD. As outlined in the model specification, these economic indicators are commonly used in traditional econometric model specification to identify the determinants of redistribution. These variables can be interpreted as reflecting economic growth and business cycles.

Fourthly, in addition to the traditional validity test on the impacts of democracy, five different hypotheses are jointly tested. Unlike the variables above, the indicators reflecting these five different hypotheses aim to test why and how the M-R hypothesis does not hold.[5] The detailed theoretical and empirical studies have been reviewed in Chapter 4.

First, the ***captured democracy hypothesis*** measures the extent to which the elite group use their wealth to capture democracy (Acemoglu et al., 2015; Scheve and Stasavage, 2017). As a proxy for this hypothesis, Acemoglu et al. (2015) use the land Gini coefficient as a proxy indicator of the elite power. However, to measure this hypothesis, it is not necessary to focus on a specific elite group. For this purpose, recent studies use the degree of political inequality, which measures the distribution of political power across voting groups. This study as a proxy of this hypothesis uses the political inequality index (PI) from the *Varieties of Democracy* ("V-Dem") (Cole, 2018; Houle, 2018; Choi, 2021). The data includes a question on "power distribution by socioeconomic position". The data are coded on a 0–4 scale to assess the extent to which the political influence of the rich, middle class, and poor are equal in given society. The highest value, 4, signifies that political influence within the society is equal.[6] To maintain consistency with other indicators, the values are reversed and normalized to a 100–0 scale, where values closer to 100 indicate greater political inequality (Choi, 2021).

Second, for the ***privatization of conflict hypothesis***, the Historical Index of Ethnic Fractionalization ("HIEF") constructed by Drazanova (2020) is utilized. Other studies employ the ethnic, linguistic, and cultural fragmentation indices of Fearon (2003) and Alesina et al. (2003) as proxies for these cleavages. However, these indices have limited coverage of countries and years. The HIEF provides ethnic fractionalization estimates for 162 countries over the years 1945–2013. The values range from 0 (no ethnic fractionalization) to 1 (each individual in a country belongs to a unique ethnic group).

Third, the ***policy regime hypothesis*** is considered to reflect the impacts of a neoliberal policy regime. For this purpose, this study uses the Index of Economic Freedom ("IEF") published by the Heritage Foundation and the Wall

Street Journal. The IEF includes 12 aspects of freedom: property rights, government integrity, judicial effectiveness, government spending, tax burden, fiscal health, business freedom, labor freedom, monetary freedom, trade freedom, investment freedom, and financial freedom. The IEF combines these 12 items into a single score with the same weights ranging from 0 (absence of neoliberalism) to 10 (complete neoliberalism). This overall score is used in the estimation.[7]

Fourth, the *government capacity hypothesis* is tested using the Corruption Perception Index (CPI) released by Transparency International. This index ranks countries based on perceived levels of public sector corruption, using expert assessments and opinion surveys on a scale of 0 (highly corrupt) to 100 (very clean). The CPI is collected by surveys from business leaders and international experts who give scores and rank countries by their perceived level of corruption in their public sectors. The data records the level of corruption ranging from a scale of zero for highly corrupt countries to a scale of 100 for very clean countries. The latest version covers until 2022 for 180 countries.

Fifth, the *interplay hypothesis between the electoral system, political system, and redistributive policy* is tested by the electoral system. Iversen and Soskice (2009) and Cruz et al. (2018) demonstrate that a proportional representation electoral system is more effective than a plurality voting system for redistribution policy. To test this hypothesis, the index on the electoral systems (plurality and proportional) of 180 countries for 1975–2017, conducted by the *Database of Political Institutions 2017*, is used (Cruz et al., 2018). The data is coded as 1 for plurality and 0 for proportional electoral system.

Table 5.1 summarizes the proxy indicators and their sources to reflect the five hypotheses.

Table 5.2 provides descriptive statistics of the variables used in the panel estimation. The number of sample period is quite diverse due to different data sources, implying different number of countries and different sample period for diverse model specifications. For example, redistribution indicator, ReD, as

Table 5.1 Five hypotheses and indicators

Hypotheses	*Proxy data and sources*
1. Captured democracy hypothesis	Political Inequality Index (PI) in the Variety of Democracy (V-DEM)
2. Privatization of conflict hypothesis	Historical Index of Ethnic Fractionalization (HIEF) of Drazanova (2020)
3. Policy regime hypothesis	Index of Economic Freedom (IEF) of the Heritage Foundation
4. Government capacity hypothesis	Corruption Perception Index (CPI) from Transparency International
5. Interplay hypothesis: electoral system, political system, and redistributive policy	Voting system (proportional representation or plurality voting system) (Plurality) in the Database of Political Institutions

Table 5.2 Descriptive statistics

Variable	*Abbreviation*	*Observation*	*Mean*	*Standard Deviation*	*Min.*	*Max.*
Redistribution	ReD	4,408	6.92	7.23	–9.4	25.9
Market Gini	$Gini^M$	4,408	45.51	6.30	28.7	72.3
GDP per capita	ln(GDP per capita)	4,213	8.48	1.45	5.25	11.63
GDP growth rate	GDP growth rate	4,218	3.52	5.08	–50.25	65
Squared GDP per capita	$[\ln(\text{GDP per capita})])^2$	4,213	74.08	24.88	27.60	135.26
Unemployment rate	Unemployment rate	4,100	7.81	5.41	0.25	31.84
=1 if BMR democracy	BMR	3,708	0.63	0.48	0	1
=1 if CGV democracy	CGV	2,629	0.62	0.48	0	1
=1 if Polity V democracy	Polity V	3,338	0.61	0.49	0	1
Political Inequality Index	PI	1,942	36.41	15.03	0	100
Historical Index of Ethnic Fractionalization	HIEF	3,039	0.44	0.25	0.004	0.89
Index of Economic Freedom	IEF	2,265	6.72	0.98	2.74	8.98
Corruption Perception Index	CPI	2,740	44.58	21.93	4	100
=1 if plurality	Plurality	4,152	0.54	0.50	0	1

a main dependent variable and market income Gini, $Gini^M$, include 4,408 samples. However, the sample size of the institutional indicators to reflect the five hypotheses are quite limited: 1,942 for the political inequality index and 2,265 for the index of economic freedom. Further, three democracy indicators have different sample size: 3,708 for the BMR democracy, 2,629 for the CGV democracy and 3,328 for the Polity V democracy. For the estimation, the BMR democracy indicator is used due to the largest sample size.

5.3 Estimation results: redistribution and democracy

Initially, the baseline model specification is estimated to test the empirical validity of the M-R hypothesis. From Equation 5.1, the panel estimation considers both market income inequality and economic factors as a benchmark model specification, then three democracy indicators are additionally considered. Through the Hausman model specification tests for all panel estimations, only fixed-effect estimation results are reported. Table 5.3 presents the fixed-effect panel estimation results based on the M-R hypothesis. Model (1) is a simple panel regression estimation result of redistribution on market income inequality, considering year dummies. The results show that the coefficient for market income inequality is positive and statistically significant. This infers that countries with higher market income inequality tend to show higher redistribution, further improving income distribution through social safety nets. This result can be interpreted to support the validity of the M-R hypothesis.

Table 5.3 Baseline panel model estimation results I

	Model (1)	*Model (2)*	*Model (3)*	*Model (4)*
$Gini^M$	0.161***	0.160***	0.112***	0.162***
	(0.007)	(0.009)	(0.012)	(0.009)
BMR		-0.084		
		(0.058)		
CGV			-0.036	
			(0.072)	
Polity V				-0.179***
				(0.058)
Constant	-0.485	-1.109***	1.037*	-0.886**
	(0.328)	(0.394)	(0.559)	(0.417)
Observations	4,408	3,708	2,629	3,338
Within R-squared	0.155	0.135	0.056	0.138
Number of countries	184	181	180	156

Notes: 1) BMR, CGV, and Polity V are democracy indices provided by Boix et al. (2013), Cheibub et al. (2018), and the Polity Dataset, respectively. $Gini^M$ is an index of market income inequality. 2) The coefficients for year dummies are not reported. 3) Robust standard errors are shown in parentheses. 4) *** Significant at the 1% level, ** Significant at the 5% level, * Significant at the 10% level

The consideration of democratic indicators does not affect the estimation result for market income inequality. The estimation coefficients for two democratic indicators, excluding Polity V, are not shown to be statistically significant. Polity V is shown to be negative and statistically significant, indicating no role of democratic indicators for redistribution. Therefore, it can be concluded that the validity of the M-R hypothesis cannot be confirmed under this baseline model specification. In other words, we cannot confirm that democratic countries achieve better performance in income redistribution than non-democratic countries.

Table 5.4 displays the fixed-effect panel estimation results by slightly extending the baseline models above, considering economic determinants that have been used in various related literature.

First, the coefficients for market income Gini are quite consistent with the results above, showing positive and significant results. This indicates that the redistribution has a positive relationship with the degree of market income inequality, supporting M-R hypothesis.

Second, two economic indicators (GDP per capita and economic growth) are shown to be statistically significant. The GDP per capita exhibits a

Table 5.4 Baseline model estimation results II

	Model (5)	*Model (6)*	*Model (7)*	*Model (8)*
$Gini^M$	0.154***	0.148***	0.082***	0.144***
	(0.008)	(0.009)	(0.013)	(0.010)
ln(GDP per capita)	-4.054***	-4.486***	-4.346***	-4.834***
	(0.376)	(0.424)	(0.521)	(0.458)
[ln(GDP per capita)]^2	0.256***	0.294***	0.326***	0.315***
	(0.024)	(0.027)	(0.033)	(0.029)
GDP growth rate	-0.018***	-0.018***	-0.017***	-0.019***
	(0.003)	(0.003)	(0.003)	(0.003)
Unemployment rate	0.031***	0.029***	-0.000	0.033***
	(0.006)	(0.006)	(0.007)	(0.007)
BMR		0.031		
		(0.060)		
CGV			0.032	
			(0.069)	
Polity V				-0.056
				(0.059)
Constant	15.164***	15.945***	15.798***	17.702***
	(1.618)	(1.809)	(2.246)	(1.951)
Observations	3,993	3,343	2,335	3,103
R-squared	0.212	0.186	0.128	0.190
Number of countries	166	163	160	149

Notes: 1) BMR, CGV, and Polity V are democracy indices provided by Boix et al. (2013), Cheibub et al. (2018), and the Polity Dataset, respectively. $Gini^M$ is an index of market income inequality. 2) The coefficients for year dummies are not reported. 3) Robust standard errors are shown in parentheses. 4) *** Significant at the 1% level, ** Significant at the 5% level, * Significant at the 10% level non-linear U-shaped relationship with redistribution. The coefficients for the economic growth rate are negative and statistically significant. This suggests that higher economic growth does not necessarily promote income redistribution. It can be inferred that a higher economic growth rate leads to worsening market income inequality, and thus the government does not play a significant role in redistribution. For the unemployment rate, the estimated coefficients, except *CGV*, are positive and statistically significant. This suggests that social welfare policies, including the tax system and social transfers, contribute to improving income distribution. In particular, unemployment insurance is one of the representative policies. Therefore, it can be inferred that the estimation results of the extended model specifications, with consideration of economic indicators, do not support the role of democracies for redistribution, reflecting no validity of the M-R hypothesis.

From Tables 5.3 and 5.4 as baseline model specifications with consideration of market income inequality and economic indicators, democracy does not contribute to increase the size of redistribution, indicating no validity of democratic states for the M-R hypothesis. Therefore, it will be useful to examine why the M-R hypothesis does not hold. For this purpose, this study considers five different hypotheses.

5.4 Estimation results: M-L hypothesis for democratic countries

In addition to the model specifications above, the interaction terms between market income inequality and the five hypotheses are considered. This is to test why and how the M-R hypothesis does not hold. In Chapter 4, the five main hypotheses based on a diverse literature review are examined. The comparison between the relation of redistribution and market income inequality in Figure 5.3 shows two distinct trends over market income inequality values, even for democratic countries. However, there is no strong trend between redistribution and market income inequality for non-democratic countries. Thus, we test the validity of the M-R hypothesis only for democratic countries. The model specification in Equation 5.2 is used for estimation. The estimations are undertaken only for the BMR indicator that covers the longest period (1800–2022). The estimation results with other democratic indicators are consistent with those of the BMR.

To examine the impacts of the five hypotheses, more detailed and extended model specifications are estimated. Tables 5.5 and 5.6 present the estimation results for two extended model specifications. Table 5.5 tests the respective impacts of the indicators that reflect the five hypotheses explained in Chapter 4. Table 5.6 presents the estimation results of the interaction terms between market income inequality and the five indicators reflecting five hypotheses. Table 5.6 also tests both the indicators of the five hypotheses and their interaction terms with market income inequalities.

From Table 5.5, the coefficients for market income inequality are shown to be positive and statistically significant, which are quite consistent with those of

Table 5.5 Extended model estimation results I

	Model (9)	*Model (10)*	*Model (11)*	*Model (12)*	*Model (13)*
Gini^M	0.200***	0.161***	0.163***	0.170***	0.169***
	(0.014)	(0.014)	(0.014)	(0.013)	(0.012)
ln(GDP per capita)	-3.183***	-6.281***	-0.378	-2.328**	-5.853***
	(1.094)	(0.989)	(1.058)	(1.008)	(0.730)
[ln(GDP per capita)]^2	0.178***	0.355***	0.017	0.124**	0.328***
	(0.064)	(0.057)	(0.061)	(0.059)	(0.043)
GDP growth rate	0.004	-0.007	0.004	0.002	-0.002
	(0.008)	(0.006)	(0.006)	(0.006)	(0.005)
Unemployment rate	0.038***	0.043***	0.064***	0.060***	0.049***
	(0.011)	(0.010)	(0.010)	(0.010)	(0.008)
PI	-0.024***				
	(0.005)				
HIEF		0.344			
		(0.975)			
IEF			-0.410***		
			(0.065)		
CPI				-0.010**	
				(0.004)	
Plurality					-0.193*
					(0.117)
Constant	16.001***	27.562***	5.219	11.615**	25.421***
	(5.082)	(4.700)	(4.748)	(4.582)	(3.375)
Observations	1,410	1,648	1,413	1,564	2,070
R-squared	0.345	0.264	0.290	0.285	0.295
Number of countries	64	90	100	104	109

Notes: 1) *Gini^M* are indices that represent the levels of market income inequality, political inequality, and economic freedom, respectively. 2) *PI*, HIEF, and *IEF* are indices that represent the levels of market income inequality, political inequality, and economic freedom, respectively. 3) The coefficients for year and country dummies are not reported. 4) Standard errors are shown in parentheses. 5) *** Significant at the 1% level, ** Significant at the 5% level, * Significant at the 10% level

the previous baseline model specifications. Economic indicators show similar results, except for GDP growth rate. GDP per capita and its squared term are statistically significant negative and positive, respectively. Unemployment rate is statistically significant and positive. They are consistent with those of the baseline models. However, the coefficients for unemployment for all models are not shown to be significant, inconsistently with the results of baseline model estimation.

The indicators that reflect the five different hypotheses have negative and statistically significant coefficients except for the Historical Index of Ethnic Fractionalization (HIEF). For the first hypothesis indicator, the negative coefficient for

Table 5.6 Extended model estimation results II

	Model (14)	*Model (15)*	*Model (16)*	*Model (17)*	*Model (18)*
$Gini^M$	0.222***	0.190***	0.210***	0.170***	0.171***
	(0.015)	(0.017)	(0.018)	(0.014)	(0.012)
ln(GDP per capita)	-3.196***	-7.462***	-0.883	-2.782***	-5.851***
	(1.093)	(0.976)	(1.057)	(1.006)	(0.729)
[ln(GDP per capita)]^2	0.182***	0.415***	0.040	0.142**	0.328***
	(0.064)	(0.056)	(0.061)	(0.059)	(0.043)
GDP growth rate	0.003	-0.007	0.004	0.003	-0.002
	(0.008)	(0.006)	(0.006)	(0.006)	(0.005)
Unemployment rate	0.038***	0.043***	0.063***	0.061***	0.049***
	(0.011)	(0.010)	(0.010)	(0.010)	(0.008)
$Gini^M$ × PI	-0.060***				
	(0.011)				
$Gini^M$ × HIEF		-0.067***			
		(0.019)			
$Gini^M$ × IEF			-0.007***		
			(0.001)		
$Gini^M$ × CPI				-0.000	
				(0.000)	
$Gini^M$ × Plurality					-0.005**
					(0.003)
Constant	14.957***	33.118***	5.073	13.707***	25.306***
	(5.064)	(4.527)	(4.869)	(4.607)	(3.367)
Observations	1,410	1,648	1,413	1,564	2,070
R-squared	0.347	0.270	0.282	0.282	0.296
Number of countries	64	90	100	104	109

Notes: 1) $Gini^M$ are indices that represent the levels of market income inequality, political inequality, and economic freedom, respectively. 2) *PI*, HIEF, and *IEF* are indices that represent the levels of market income inequality, political inequality, and economic freedom, respectively. 3) The coefficients for year and country dummies are not reported. 4) Standard errors are shown in parentheses. 5) *** Significant at the 1% level, ** Significant at the 5% level, * Significant at the 10% level

political inequality indicator, PI, indicates that higher political inequality leads to less degree of income redistribution. The positive coefficient for the IEF presents that the more liberal countries show higher redistribution, indicating that liberal countries tend to adopt better social welfare policies and pro-poor tax and transfer policies with improved income inequality. And the negative and significant coefficient for the electoral system with 1 for a plurality system confirms that a proportional representation electoral system is more effective than a plurality voting system for redistribution policy. However, the negative and significant coefficient for CPI is not consistent with our expectation, indicating that cleaner countries are less income redistribution.

Table 5.6 presents the estimation results for the extended model specifications with interaction terms between the hypothesis indicators and market income inequality. The model is to examine joint effect of two indicators, i.e., effects of a specific institution assuming that the market income inequality is given. For example, positive coefficient for a specific interaction term, assuming market income inequality is given, indicates that in democratic countries, the greater the institutional indicator is, the more income is redistributed.

The coefficient for the interaction term between PI and market income inequality is negative and statistically significant, confirming the captured democracy hypothesis as Table 5.5. In other words, the higher political inequality in the form of wealth, race and ethnicity etc. is, the less income tends to be redistributed. The negative and statistically significant coefficient for the interaction term between HIEF and market income inequality to reflect the privatization of conflict hypothesis indicates that the higher ethnic fractionalization is, the less income redistributed. The estimation result for the interaction term between IEF and market income inequality is consistent with our expectation, confirming the policy regime hypothesis. And the estimation result for the Plurality is consistent with the hypothesis and the result in Table 5.5. However, the coefficient for CPI and market income inequality as a government capacity hypothesis is not statistically significant. It can be in contrast with the result of Table 5.5 with negative and significant estimation coefficient for CPI alone. Therefore, it is not consistent with our expectation.

From the estimation results of two extended model specifications, Tables 5.5 and 5.6, the following implications for democratic countries are derived.

Firstly, the coefficients for market income inequality align with those in Tables 5.3 and 5.4, confirming that higher market income inequalities lead to increased income redistribution. Therefore, it can be inferred that the M-R hypothesis is well confirmed through various estimation model estimations.

Secondly, the estimation results for economic indicators are also consistent with the results of previous findings. There is an inverted U-shaped relation between GDP per capita and redistribution. The unemployment rate contributes to increased income redistribution, emphasizing the role of government in implementing social safety net policies. However, the economic growth rate does not play a statistically significant role in changing redistribution.

Thirdly, there are intriguing estimation results on the five hypotheses that show why and how the M-R hypotheses do not hold in democratic countries.

i) The political inequality (PI) reflecting the captured democracy hypothesis shows a negative and significant coefficient in Table 5.5. The interaction term with market income inequality in Table 5.6 is negative and statistically significant, confirming the captured democracy hypothesis.
ii) The Index of Economic Freedom (IEF) for the policy regime hypothesis shows a negative and statistically significant coefficient in Table 5.5, and its interaction term with market income inequality is shown to be negative and statistically significant in Table 5.6.

iii) The Corruption Perception Index (*CPI*) for the ***government capacity hypothesis*** shows a negative and statistically significant coefficient in Table 5.5, while the interaction term with market income inequality in Table 5.6 is not significant. Therefore, the CPI indicator does not play a significant role in explaining the government capacity hypothesis.
iv) The dummy Plurality for the voting system reflects ***the interplay hypothesis between the electoral system, political system, and redistributive policy***. It is recorded as a value of 1 for a plurality voting system and 0 for other electoral systems (proportional representation systems). The coefficient for Plurality shows a negative and statistically significant result, which is consistent with the finding of Iversen and Soskice (2009). They suggest that income redistribution is more effectively achieved under proportional representation systems or mixed systems than under plurality voting systems.

The estimation results for the five hypotheses suggest that the greater the institution indicator in indicators of political inequality, and social conflict, the less income is distributed. Additionally, the plurality voting system tends to distribute less income. However, the corruption perception index is not consistent with our expectation.

5.5 Conclusion

This chapter utilizes panel data for income inequality and democratic indicators, along with economic variables, to apply fixed-effect panel estimation in investigating the validity of the M-R hypotheses.

The estimation results can be summarized as follows:

Firstly, market income inequality has a strong, positive, and statistically significant coefficient across all model specifications. This result aligns with the original M-R hypothesis, which posits that higher market income inequality leads to a higher degree of redistribution.

Secondly, the economic indicators, assumed to be the main determinants in the related literature, are largely consistent with the estimation results, except for economic growth rate which is not statistically significant. Therefore, economic growth and business cycle are closely related with income redistribution.

Thirdly, variations exist between democratic and non-democratic countries. For non-democratic countries, there is no significant correlation between redistribution and market income inequality. However, democratic countries display a positive relationship, albeit with two distinct trends. Therefore, it is inferred that democratic system itself cannot guarantee increase of income redistribution, improving disposable income distribution.

Fourthly, the fixed-effect panel estimation results reveals that the values of the five indicators, reflecting the five hypotheses, are strongly related to redistribution given market income distribution. Only the corruption perception index (CPI) shows inconsistent results with our expectation.

> Therefore, it can be concluded that the five main hypotheses, reviewed from the related literature, confirm why and how the M-R hypothesis does not hold, even in democratic countries.

Through graphical and estimation analyses, it is concluded that the M-R hypothesis is well confirmed in terms of the strong positive relationship between redistribution and market income inequality. However, the democratic system does not consistently align with the M-R hypothesis, as the relationship displays two distinct patterns, suggesting other factors for confirming the M-R hypothesis. For this purpose, five main hypotheses explaining why the M-R hypothesis does not hold are tested through a comprehensive literature review and panel estimation. The proxy factors reflecting these hypotheses are chosen through comprehensive literature review and the data with larger country and year coverage are selected.

Based on our estimation results, certain conditions should be fostered to improve income redistribution in democratic countries. These conditions extend beyond the establishment of formal democratic institutions, such as a multi-party political system, universal adult suffrage, and regularly contested elections. Democratic societies must also effectively control attempts by the wealthy to leverage their wealth to influence the political sphere. In other words, the focus should be on removing big money from politics and strengthening political participation and expression of opinions among low-income groups who lack political resources. Additionally, it is crucial to diminish discrimination based on race, religion, gender, and other factors. Moreover, the electoral system must guarantee fair representation of the demands of different societal segments. Finally, new policy regimes capable of achieving a balance between efficiency and equity are required.

Appendix 5.1 Question and responses of the survey on the power distribution by socio-economic position

Question: Is political power distributed according to socio-economic position?

Clarification: All societies are characterized by some degree of economic (wealth and income) inequality. In some societies, income and wealth are distributed in a grossly unequal fashion. In others, the difference between rich and poor is not so great. Here, we are concerned not with the degree of social inequality but rather with the political effects of this inequality. Specifically, we are concerned with the extent to which wealth and income translates into political power.

Responses:

0: Wealthy people enjoy a virtual monopoly on political power. Average and poorer people have almost no influence.

1: Wealthy people have a very strong hold on political power. People of average income have little say. Poorer people have essentially no influence.

2: Wealthy people have a very strong hold on political power. People of average or poorer income have some degree of influence but only on issues that matter less for wealthy people.
3: Wealthy people have more political power than others. But people of average income have almost as much influence and poor people also have a significant degree of political power.
4: Wealthy people have no more political power than those whose economic status is average or poor. Political power is more or less equally distributed across economic groups.

Appendix 5.2 Questions and responses of the alternative indicators of *Policy Regime Change*

The *Economic Left-Right Scale Indicator* provided by *Varieties of Party Identity and Organization* (V-Party Dataset) can be utilized as a substitute proxy variable for the policy regime hypothesis. The question and responses for the data are as follows.

Question: Please locate the party in terms of its overall ideological stance on economic issues.

Clarification: Parties on the economic left want government to play an active role in the economy. This includes higher taxes, more regulation and government spending and a more generous welfare state. Parties on the economic right emphasize a reduced economic role for government: privatization, lower taxes, less regulation, less government spending, and a leaner welfare state.

Responses: 0: Far-left; 1: Left; 2: Center-left; 3: Center; 4: Center-right; 5: Right;6: Far-right.

Appendix 5.3 Description and measures of three democracy indicators

Three democracy measures used in the estimation in Chapter 5 are explained in detail, which are BMR democracy, CGV democracy, and Polity V democracy, respectively. First, the BMR democracy proposed by Boix et al. (2012, 2013, "BMR") during the 1800–2020 period defines a country as democratic if it meets clear standards for both contestation and participation. That is, a democratic country should elect political leaders through free and fair elections (contestation) and satisfy a threshold value of suffrage (participation). Specifically, for the contestation criteria, the legislature should be elected in free and fair elections, and the executive should be elected in majority elections and be directly accountable to the voters or to the legislature (Boix et al., 2013). For the participation criteria, BMR democracy requires a minimal level of suffrage, which means requiring a majority of adult males to have the right to vote.

Second, the CGV democracy proposed by Cheibub et al. (2009, 2010, "CGV") during 1946–2008 defines a country as democratic if the country obeys the following criteria. First, the country should use direct election system such as popular vote in executive selection. Also, the mode of legislative selection should be elective, and the status of legislature should be elected. That is, the country should have elective legislature so that the legislators are elected by means of either direct or indirect popular election, and not closed nor appointed. Furthermore, the legislature should include members from multiple parties. In addition, the country should not only legally allow multiple parties, but multiple parties should be in presence. Moreover, the country should have multiple parties outside of regime front and not belonging to regime front. Further, the incumbents in democratic regime should not consolidate the incumbent advantage, that is, they should not unconstitutionally close the lower house of the national legislature or rewrote the rules in their favor. One of the examples of the consolidation of incumbent advantage is Argentine provincial elections in 2019 (Suárez-Cao, 2021). Finally, albeit the

Table A-5.1 Polity V democracy measures criteria

Criteria	*Democracy value*	*Autocracy value*
Competitiveness of executive recruitment		
(1) Election	+2	
(2) Transitional	+1	
(3) Selection		+2
Openness of executive recruitment		
(1) Dual/election	+1	
(2) Election	+1	
(3) Closed		+1
(4) Dual/designation		+1
Constraint on chief executive		
(1) Executive parity or subordination	+4	
(2) Intermediate category	+3	
(3) Substantial limitations	+2	
(4) Intermediate category	+1	
(5) Unlimited authority		+3
(6) Intermediate category		+2
(7) Slight to moderate limitations		+1
Competitiveness of (political) participation		
(1) Competitive	+3	
(2) Transitional	+2	
(3) Factional	+1	
(4) Repressed		+2
(5) Suppressed		+1
Regulation of participation		
(1) Restricted		+2
(2) Sectarian		+1
Total	0–10	0–10

Source: Author reconstructed based on Marshall and Gurr (2020).

country holds multi-party executive and legislative elections, it could be identified as dictatorship regime if the present office knows the opposition party can't win or the opposition party are not allowed to win. Cheibub et al. (2009) refers this case as violating the "alternation" rule.

Third, the Polity V democracy proposed by Marshall and Gurr (2020, "Polity V") during 1800–2018 scores the regime democracy level between −10 (worst, full autocracy) to +10 (best, fully democracy), and the regimes that score over 5 are classified as democratic. The score is estimated by subtracting the autocracy value (0–10) from the democracy value (0–10). Democracy value is measured by using the following criteria: competitiveness of executive recruitment (0–2), openness of executive recruitment (0–1), constraint on chief executive (0–4), and competitiveness of political participation (0–3). Whereas autocracy value is measured by using the following criteria: competitiveness of executive recruitment (0–2), openness of executive recruitment (0–1), constraint on chief executive (0–3), regulation of participation (0–2), and competitiveness of participation (0–2). For example, if the executive recruitment mode is election, the regime earns +2, if the mode is transitional, the regime earns +1, if the mode is selection, then the regime earns −2 for total polity score. Refer to Table A-5.1 for detailed Polity V democracy measures criteria.

References

Boix, C., Miller M. K., Rosato, S. (2022), "Boix-Miller-Rosato dichotomous coding of democracy, 1800–2020," *Harvard Dataverse*, V1.

Cheibub, J. A., Gandhi, J., Vreeland, J. R. (2009), *Democracy and dictatorship revisited codebook*, University of Illinois, Urbana-Champaign, IL.

Marshall, M. G., Gurr, T. R. (2020), *Polity 5: political regime characteristics and transitions, 1800–2018, Dataset Users' Manual*, Center for Systemic Peace, Vienna, VA.

Suárez-Cao, J. (2021), "Squaring the circle: the consolidation of incumbency advantage in the Argentine provincial elections of 2019," *Regional & Federal Studies*, 31(3), pp. 313–335.

Appendix 5.4 Description and measures of five hypothesis proxy indicators

Five hypothesis proxy indicators summarized in Table 5.1 and utilized in the estimation in Chapter 5 are explained in detail: are the Polity Inequality Index (PI), the Historical Index of Ethnic Fractionalization (HIEF), the Index of Economic Freedom (IEF), the Corruption Perception Index (CPI), and the voting system, respectively.

The Polity Inequality Index (PI) is a comprehensive cross-national measure of political inequality using datasets from Varieties of Democracy (V-DEM). It is mainly based on the two distinct dimensions of participation and representation in the Democratic Performance Index (DPI) considering a middle-range conception (Equality of Opportunity) (Choi, 2021). The ordinal ratings range from 0 to 4, where the higher grade indicates the higher level of equality. To measure the level of inequality, it has been reversed and normalized with 0–100 scale, where 100 indicates the highest level of inequality. However, the maximum value of 100 does not mean perfect inequality (Choi, 2019).

The Historical Index of Ethnic Fractionalization (HIEF) dataset contains an ethnic fractionalization index for 162 countries from 1945 to 2013. The original data on ethnic group was garnered from the Composition of Religious and Ethnic Groups (CREG) project implemented by the Cline Center for Democracy. The level of ethnic fractionalization has been calculated based on the annual percentage of ethnic groups using Herfindahl concentration index (Drazanova, 2020). It ranges from 0 to 1, where 1 indicates that each individual is from different ethnic groups while 0 indicates that all individuals are in the same ethnic groups.

The Index of Economic Freedom (IEF), developed by the Heritage Foundation, consists of twelve aspects of freedom: property rights, government integrity, judicial effectiveness, government spending, tax burden, fiscal health, business freedom, labor freedom, monetary freedom, trade freedom, investment freedom, and financial freedom. It covers 184 sovereign countries from 1995 to 2023. These aspects are classified into four broad categories: rule of law, government size, regulatory efficiency, and open markets. Each indicator is graded on a scale of 0 to 100 and an overall score is calculated by equally averaging these twelve economic freedoms (Kim, 2023). The greater score a country has, the better the country's economic freedom is.

The Corruption Perception Index (CPI) published by the Transparency International measures 180 countries and territories by their perceived level of corruption. It ranges from 0 to 100, where 100 means very clean and 0 means highly corrupted. The institution has collected 13 different data sources from 12 different indicators and standardized by subtracting the mean and dividing by the standard deviation of each source in the baseline year from each country score (Transparency International, 2023). Each country's score is calculated by an average of all standardized scores available for that country.

To measure a voting system of each country, Database of Political Institutions (DPI, 2017) from IDB was used. It covers 180 countries from 1975 to 2017. As a proxy of electoral system, respondents are asked about their countries' electoral rule, whether candidates are elected based on the percent of votes received by their party and/or if our sources specifically call the system "proportional representation" (Cruz et al., 2018). If the answer is yes, it scores 1 as a dummy variable, and otherwise 0.

References

Choi, G. (2019), *Political inequality index*, Ann Arbor, MI: Inter-university Consortium for Political and Social Research [distributor].

Kim, A.B. (2023), *2023 Index of economic freedom*, The Heritage Foundation, Washington, DC.

Transparency International. (2023), *Corruption perception index 2022 report*. Transparency International, Berlin.

Appendix 5.5

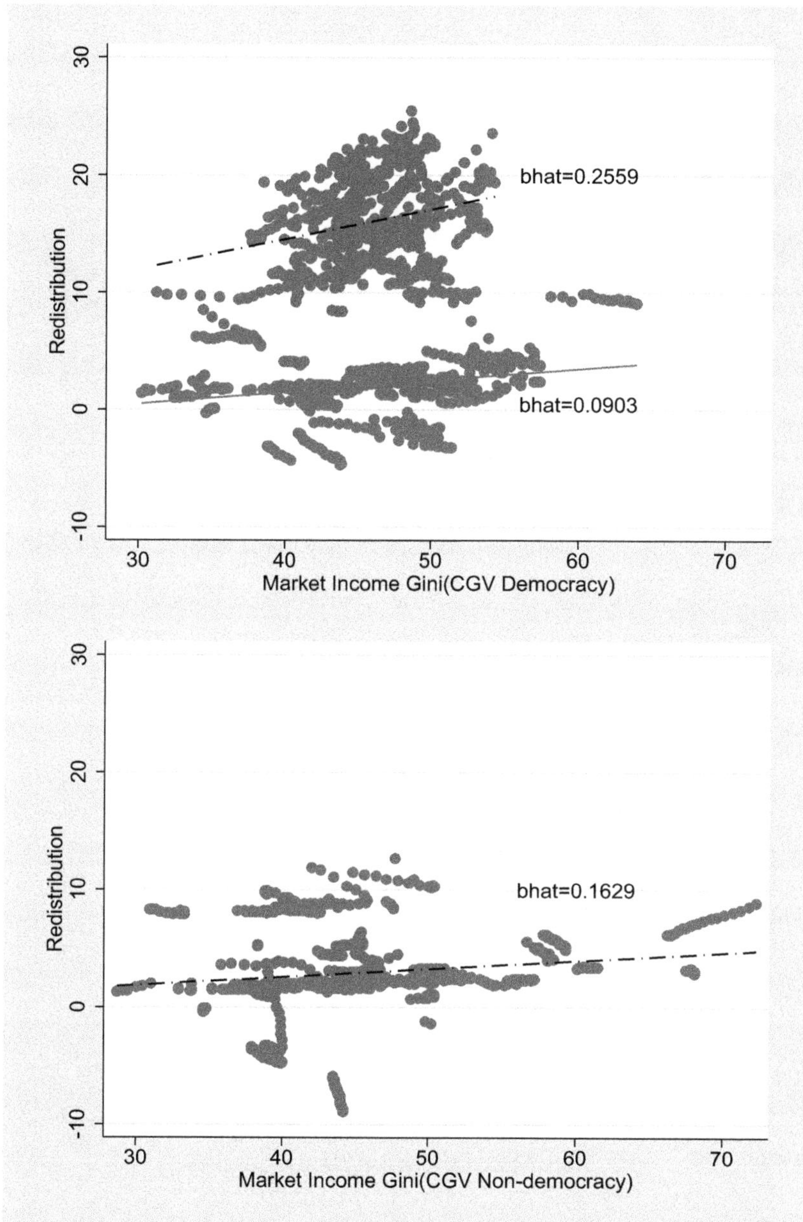

Figure A-5.1 Market income inequality and redistribution according to CGV democracy

Note: 1) Redistribution is calculated as the difference between market and disposable income inequality.
2) bhat is the estimation coefficient for the regression of redistribution on market income inequality.

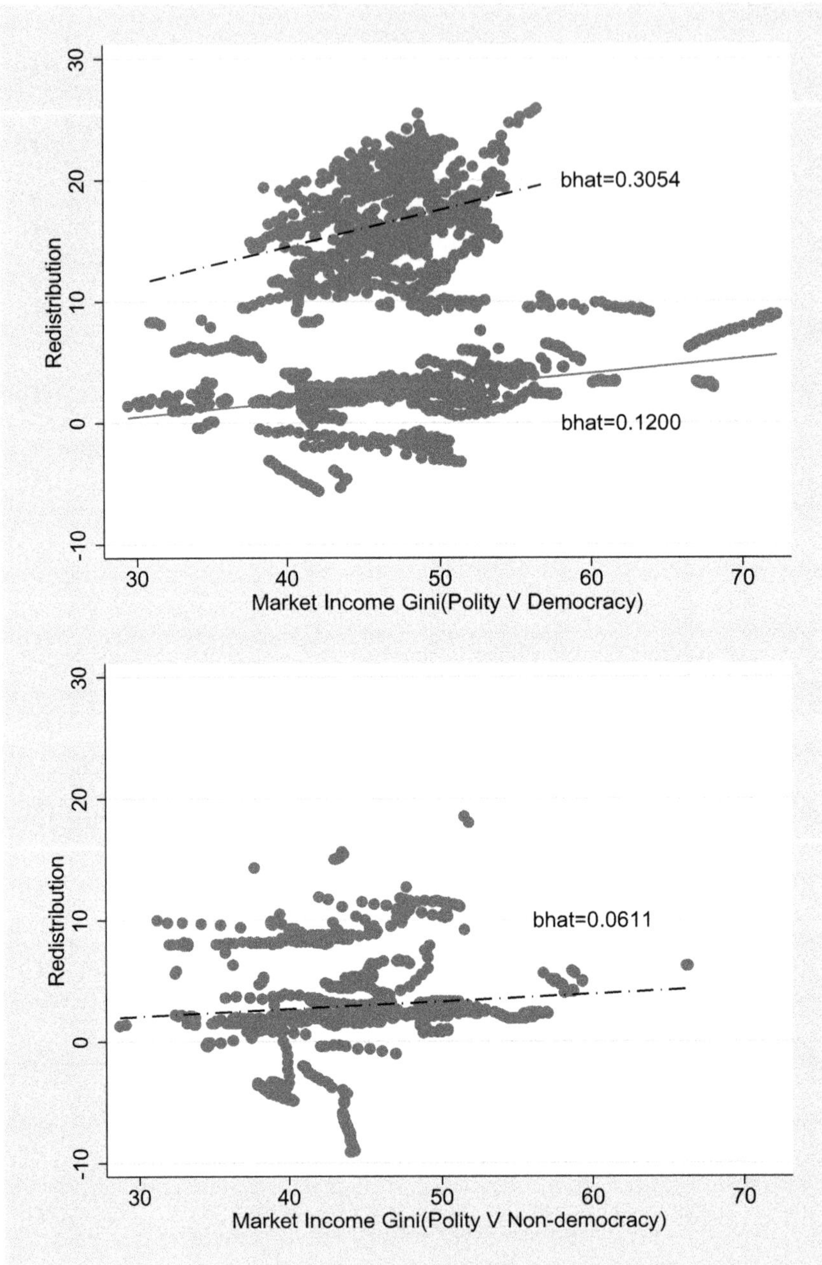

Figure A-5.2 Market income inequality and redistribution by Polity V democracy

Note: 1) Redistribution is calculated as the difference between market and disposable income inequality.

2) bhat is the estimation coefficient for the regression of redistribution on market income inequality.

Notes

1 Especially, GDP per capita and its squared term are used in testing the validity of the inverted U-shaped Kuznets hypothesis. According to the hypothesis, the income inequality increases and then decreased as the economy develops. For testing the hypothesis, the dependent variable should be market income or disposable income inequality. Therefore, it is carefully interpreted for the estimated coefficients of two variables.
2 See Appendix 5.3 for more detailed description of the three democracy measures.
3 The correlation coefficients among the three democratic indicators are as follows: 0.8407 for BMR and CGV, 0.8421 for BMR and Polity V, and 0.7534 for CGV and Polity V. Furthermore, the correlation coefficients between market income Gini and democratic indicators are not strong, with 0.19992 with BMR, 0.0840 with CGV, and 0.2555 with Polity V.
4 The other two democratic indicators (CGV and Polity V) yield similar patterns. Refer to Appendix Figures A-5.1 and A-5.2.
5 See Appendix 5.4 for more detailed description of the five hypotheses' proxy indicators.
6 The detailed explanation of questions and responses from the survey is summarized in Appendix 5.1.
7 The IEF can be replaced by another indicator, the *Economic Left-Right Scale Indicator by Varieties of Party Identity and Organization* (V-Party Dataset), since IEF reflects the issue of neoliberalism rather than the impact of the policy regime (Seo and Kang, 2023). This data provides information on the lower chamber's party seat distribution in elections and ideological stances on economic issues for political parties in each country. Seo and Kang (2023) define the policy similarity between parties as the absolute difference in positions of economic policies between the first party and the second party. In this definition, smaller absolute values indicate higher policy similarity due to similar economic policies. While this data is more suitable than IEF for the *policy regime hypothesis*, the coverage of data on year and countries is too limited. The estimation results are shown to be significant only for the "CGV". Refer to Appendix 5.2 for questions and responses of the data.

References

Acemoglu, D., Naidu, S., Restrepo, P., and Robinson, J.A. (2015), "Democracy, redistribution, and inequality," (eds.) Atkinson, A. B., Bourguignon, F.), *Handbook of Income Distribution*, pp. 1885–1966, North-Holland: Elsevier.

Alesina, A., Devleeschauwer, A., Easterly, W., Kurlat, S., Wacziarg, R. (2003), "Fractionalization," *Journal of Economic Growth*, 8(2), pp. 155–194.

Boix, C., M. Miller, and S. Rosato. (2013), "A Complete Dataset of Political Regimes, 1800–2007". *Comparative Political Studies* 46(12), pp. 1523–1554. https://doi.org/10.1177/0010414012463905. Available at https://dataverse.harvard.edu/dataset.xhtml?persistentId=doi:10.7910/DVN/FJLMKT (versions 1–3) and https://sites.google.com/site/mkmtwo/data (version 4.0), retrieved on September 20, 2023.

Cheibub, José Antonio, Jennifer Gandhi, and James Raymond Vreeland. 2010. "Democracy and Dictatorship Revisited." *Public Choice*, 143(2–1), pp. 67–101. https://sites.google.com/site/joseantoniocheibub/datasets/democracy-and-dictatorship-revisited, retrieved on May 1, 2020.

Choi, G. (2021), "Conceptualizing and measuring political inequality in a cross-national perspective," *Comparative Sociology*, 20, pp. 1–44.

Cole, W.M. (2018), "Poor and powerless: Economic and political inequality in cross-national perspective, 1981–2011," *International Sociology*, 33(3), pp. 357–385.

Cruz, C., Keefer, P., Scartascini, C. (2018), *Database of political institutions 2017*, Inter-American Development Bank, Washington, DC.
Database of Political Institutions 2017, https://publications.iadb.org/en/database-political-institutions-2017-dpi2017, retrieved on May 1, 2020.
Drazanova, L. (2020), "Introducing the Historical Index of Ethnic Fractionalization (HIEF) dataset: Accounting for longitudinal changes in ethnic diversity," *Journal of Open Humanities Data*, 6(1), pp. 1–8.
Fearon, J. D. (2003), "Ethnic and cultural diversity by country," *Journal of Economic Growth*, 8(2), pp. 195–222
Ferreira, F.H., Lustig, N., Teles, D. (2015), "Appraising cross-national income inequality database: An introduction," *The Journal of Economic Inequality*, 13(4), pp. 497–526.
Gründler, K., Köllner, S. (2017), "Determinants of governmental redistribution: Income distribution, development levels, and the role of perceptions," *Journal of Comparative Economics*, 45(4), pp. 930–962.
Heritage Foundation's Index of Economic Freedom, https://www.heritage.org/index/, retrieved on May 1, 2020.
HIEF (Historical Index of Ethnic Fractionalization), https://doi.org/10.7910/DVN/4JQRCL, retrieved on May 20, 2020.
Houle, C. (2018), "Does economic inequality breed political inequality?" *Democratization*, 25(8), pp. 1500–1518.
Jenkins, S. (2015), "World income inequality database: An assessment of WIID and SWIID," *The Journal of Economic Inequality*, 13(4), pp. 629–671.
Kammas, P., Sarantides, V. (2019), "Do dictatorships redistribute more?" *Journal of Comparative Economics*, 47(1), pp. 176–195.
Milanovic, B. (2010), "Four critiques of the redistribution hypothesis: An assessment," *European Journal of Political Economy*, 26(1), pp. 147–154.
Polity V (Polity V of the Polity Data Series). http://www.systemicpeace.org/inscrdata.html, retrieved on May 1, 2020.
Scervini, F. (2012), "Empirics of the median voter: democracy, redistribution and the role of middle class," *Journal of Economic Inequality*, 10(4), pp. 529–550.
Scheve, K., Stasavage, D. (2017), "Wealth inequality and democracy," *Annual Review of Political Science*, 20, pp. 451–468.
Seo, H. J., Kang, S. J. (2023), "Validity of the Meltzer and Richard hypotheses under captured democracy and policy regime hypotheses," mimeo.
Solt, Frederick. (2020), "Measuring Income Inequality Across Countries and Over Time: The Standardized World Income Inequality Database." *Social Science Quarterly* 101(3), pp. 1183–1199. SWIID Version 9.5, June 2023.
SWIID (The Standardized World Income Inequality Database). https://doi.org/10.7910/DVN/LM4OWF, retrieved on September 20, 2023.
UNU-WIDER, 2022, World Income Inequality Database (WIID). Version 30 June 2022. https://doi.org/10.35188/UNU-WIDER/WIID-300622
V-Dem dataset (Varieties of Democracy Database), https://www.v-dem.net/vdemds.html, retrieved on December 10, 2022.
V-Party dataset (Varieties of Party Identity and Organization). https://www.v-dem.net/data/v-party-dataset/, retrieved on May 28, 2023.
World Bank WDI (World Development Indicators), https://databank.worldbank.org/source/world-development-indicators, retrieved on September 20, 2023.
World Inequality Database, https://wid.world/data/, retrieved on September 20, 2023.

6 Conclusion

6.1 Summary of the research findings

The main research results of this book, as depicted in Figure 1.5 introduced in Chapter 1, can be summarized as follows.

In Chapter 2, we focus on economic area ***A***, examining the trajectory of income inequality. Additionally, we explore trends in political inequality within political area ***D***, along with inequality of opportunity. Our analysis delves into understanding the intricate relationship between income inequality, political inequality, and inequality of opportunity. Furthermore, we investigate how the political and economic domains interact through the dynamics of inequality. We categorize the respective inequalities into three types: income inequality, political inequality, and inequality of opportunity. We study these inequalities in both democratic and non-democratic countries and examine their worldwide trends. Additionally, we analyze the relationships between these three types of inequalities using cross-national data and modeling. Therefore, the primary objective of this chapter is to analyze cumulative causal relationships among various types of inequality to explain processes through which multiple inequalities are concurrently rising in the world today.

Over the past 40 years, changes in income inequality levels have been measured using the after-tax Gini coefficient and the share of the top 1% in national income in most OECD countries, indicating an increase in income inequality. In contrast, Latin American countries still show high levels of income inequality, but it appears that income inequality has transitioned from an increasing trend to a decreasing one over the past 40 years. When estimating income inequality levels using the after-tax Gini coefficient, Belgium and France are exceptional in showing a decrease over the past 40 years. Looking at the share of the top 1% in national income as of 2020, the United States shows 17.9%, Mexico 26.8%, Russia 23.8%, and Chile 22.8%, demonstrating high levels of income inequality. Political inequality levels are estimated using the V-Dem Database in two ways. First, an index estimates political inequality by examining to what extent political power is influenced by socio-economic status. Second, another index measures the extent to which political power is

DOI: 10.4324/9781032695754-6

influenced not only by socio-economic status but also by other various factors such as gender, religion, and race. In the case of the first index, over the past 20 years, political inequality has increased in 23 out of 36 OECD countries. The increase is observed in the United Kingdom, Japan, South Korea, Canada, Germany, Italy, and Nordic countries. The results of the second index show an increase in political inequality in the United States, South Korea, Canada, and Nordic countries. The extent of opportunity inequality was measured using *The Great Gatsby Curve* proposed by Corak (2013). The findings indicated that the higher the income inequality level of the parents' generation, the greater the influence of parental income on children's income. When measuring the degree of influence of parental income on children's income, it was found that in the United States, the United Kingdom, and Italy, about 50% of the advantage of the parent generation was passed on to the child generation. Opportunity inequality, as measured by Ferreira and Peragine (2015), also showed high levels in Italy, the United States, and the United Kingdom. Additionally, a high correlation between political inequality and income inequality was confirmed. By utilizing statistical data, a close relationship between income inequality, political inequality, and opportunity inequality was confirmed. Through modeling, the interrelatedness of these three forms of inequality was analyzed. It was shown that political power is practically influenced by income inequality, and income inequality and opportunity inequality are related as parental income is transmitted to children's income through human capital accumulation. Furthermore, political power influences the distribution of resources needed for human capital accumulation. The model showed that these three forms of inequality cumulatively increase through such interactions.

Chapter 3 elaborated on the M-R perspective, which suggests that the problem of income inequality can be addressed through political intervention in the economic domain. In other words, we presented a model that explained the ***D*** process of Figure 1.5. M-R argued that in democratic countries where voting rights are equally distributed among citizens, if income inequality increases, citizens will vote for parties that support income redistribution policies, thereby addressing income inequality issues. We differentiated between autocracy and democracy using a model composed of three strata: the high-income group, the middle-income group, and the low-income group. In addition, within democracy, we distinguished between cases where the middle-income group constitutes a majority, as in Director's law, and cases where the middle-income group only forms a majority when allied with the low-income group, as in M-R. Furthermore, we presented recent empirical research findings concerning the M-R model. While some studies, such as those by Simpson (1990) and Rodrik (1999), support the M-R hypothesis, the majority of research findings do not. In particular, research results suggest that income redistribution is more actively pursued in relatively more equitable countries compared to highly unequal countries, a phenomenon known as the Robin Hood Paradox. This entirely contradicts the M-R hypothesis.

In Chapter 4, our investigation aimed to uncover the reasons why the ***D*** process in Figure 1.5 does not function effectively within political area ***C*** in Figure 1.5. Moreover, it was pointed out that the M-R hypothesis failed to grasp how increased economic inequality could translate into increased political inequality. Essentially, the study highlighted that due to a limited understanding of the ***B*** process in Figure 1.5, an overly optimistic prediction was made regarding democracy's ability to easily resolve the issue of income inequality. To put it differently, if the high-income class, who has effectively converted their wealth into political power through the ***B*** process in Figure 1.5, establishes policies and systems that align with their interests, attempts to level the tilted playground in the economic area through the ***D*** process in Figure 1.5 are likely to encounter significant challenges. We presented five reasons why the equalizing effects of democracy do not work properly in the real economy, focusing on the interaction between the political and economic domains in the policy formation process: Captured democracy hypothesis; Privatization of conflict or Class betrayal voting; Policy regime; Government capacity; Election system, political system, and coalition. Furthermore, we extended the model discussed in Chapter 3 to compare these five cases. In each scenario, our research examined whether the income redistribution resulted in an increase in income inequality by comparing market income inequality and disposable income inequality. In essence, we conducted an analysis to determine whether the equalizing effects of democracy operated in these five cases. The analysis results suggest that when the higher-income class wields *de facto* political power, when there exists a higher-income class-friendly policy regime, when government corruption is extremely high, when no party represents the interests of the lower-income class, or when class betrayal voting takes place due to ideological or religious cleavages, redistribution policies can be ineffective, and may even aggravate income inequality.

Ultimately, the analysis results of Chapters 3 and 4 departed from the conventional viewpoint held by economists. Instead, they conducted an analysis that illustrated how politics is not just a matter of rhetoric but has a tangible impact on the economic domain. Furthermore, the study analyzed the transformation of income inequality into political inequality.

Using panel data for income inequality and democratic indicators, Chapter 5 conducts a graphical comparison between redistribution and market income inequality and applies fixed-effect panel estimation to test the validity of the M-R hypotheses. From a positive correlation between market income inequality and redistribution, even under simple regression, it can be inferred that the M-R hypothesis is confirmed. However, graphical comparison presents a different trend between redistribution and market income inequality, found to vary by democratic status. Democratic countries show two distinct positive relations. However, non-democratic countries do not show a significant correlation. The fixed-effect panel estimation results show that five main hypotheses, reviewed from the related literature, confirm why and how the M-R hypothesis does not hold, even under democratic countries.

6.2 How can we establish a Goldilocks balance between economic power and political power?

In Chapter 4, five reasons were presented for why the equalizing effects of democracy do not function properly (see Table 6.1). In this section, based on this analysis, we aim to explain the policy alternatives focused on how democracy can address income inequality issues through income redistribution policies.

In Chapter 4, we conducted an in-depth exploration into five diagnoses that shed light on the obstacles facing the proper implementation of redistribution within a democratic system. These diagnoses were derived from the policy formation process. Let's now direct our focus toward the policy solution put forth by these diagnoses (refer to Table 6.2). Table 6.2 illustrates how policies should intercede in processes ***B*** and ***C*** within Figure 1.5 (***B*** and ***C*** presented in the first row of Table 6.2), utilizing insights from the five diagnoses (numbered ① **to** ⑤ in the first column of Table 6.2) expounded in Table 6.1. Through its intervention in ***B*** and ***C*** in Figure 1.5, it clarifies whether a state of balance can be restored in the economic and political domains and whether democracy can effectively tackle the issue of income redistribution.

What measures can be taken to disrupt the cycle of economic inequality and political inequality? First, Schimitt (2015), Zingales (2017), and Jacobs (2017) propose the subsequent solutions concerning ① and ④ within Table 6.1. Zingales places significant emphasis on the government's involvement in the ***B*** process shown in Figure 1.5 above to restrict the impact of economic power on the political domain. In particular, efforts should be made to reduce the influence of corporations, which represent economic power in contemporary society, on politics. It is proposed that the focus should be on driving big money out of politics, that is, to remove substantial financial influence from politics (**i** and **vii** in Table 6.2). Concretely, it is essential to improve corporate transparency through reform of corporate governance and encourage democratization within companies to address the imbalanced dynamics within their

Table 6.1 The five reasons for the M-R hypothesis's lack of validity

Reasons for the M-R hypothesis's lack of validity	*Major studies*
① Captured democracy	Schattschneider (1960), Gilens (2005), Acemoglu and Robinson (2008), Bartel (2008), Hacker and Pierson (2010), Stiglitz (2012).
②. Privatization of conflict	Schattschneider (1960), Rodrik (2014), Rodrik and Mukand (2016).
③. Policy regime	Bresser-Pereira (2014), Przeworski (2014).
④. Corruption, trust, and social capital	Rothstein (2005), Algan, Cahuc, and Sangnier (2016).
⑤. Election system, political system, and coalition	Hall and Soskice (2001), Iversen and Soskice (2009), Lijphart (2012).

Table 6.2 Alternatives for Goldilocks of economic power and political power

Figure 1.5 / *Table 6.1*	B	C
①	**(i)** - The market is needed. But we have to keep the market in place. - We have to drive big money out of politics. - Enhancing corporate transparency via corporate democratization and advancing corporate governance.	**(ii)** - Rather than constraining the political power of the affluent, political reform should focus on enhancing the political voice of the low-income class, even in the face of their limited political resources.
②	**(iii)** None	**(iv)** - In a multi-party system, given that each party's development is primarily driven by economic cleavage, the feasibility of privatizing conflicts is minimal. This underscores the argument that the challenge of redistribution should be given priority. Hence, their argument revolves around prioritizing the establishment of a framework for a consensus-driven political system that can encompass the perspectives of diverse classes through power-sharing arrangements, before delving into the formulation of intricate policies.
③	**(v)** None	**(vi)** - Underlines the inherent process of policy innovation that generates novel policy frameworks, along with the pivotal role politicians play as innovators. This entails an intellectual cohort capable of critiquing prevailing policies while introducing fresh groundbreaking concepts, political leadership adept at forging new class alliances, and the collaborative efforts of media, thereby enabling the emergence of innovative new policies. - An assembly of intellectuals proficient in critiquing prevailing policies and introducing inventive new concepts (reminiscent of Keynes' academic scribbler), adept political leadership capable of forming fresh class alliances (akin to Keynes' Madmen in authority), and the collaborative efforts of the media (resembling Hayek's Knowledge Brokers) facilitate the division of labor and cooperation that drive forward new policy innovation.

(*Continued*)

Table 6.2 (Continued)

Figure 1.5 / *Table 6.1*	B	C
④	**(vii)** - We have to drive big money out of politics. - Enhancing corporate transparency via corporate democratization and advancing corporate governance.	**(viii)** None
⑤	**(ix)** None	**(x)** - Let's initiate political system reform: Implementation of a proportional representation and multi-party system.

internal structures. Moreover, to curb the influence of corporations in the political domain, there should be limitations on the amount of financial support corporations can provide to the political realm. Additionally, media and academia, which often rationalize the expansion of corporate influence, must strive to maintain their independence from corporate influence. While Zingales' perspective aims to curtail the influence of the affluent class, Jacobs and Schmitt take a different approach. On the opposing side, they propose that efforts need to be made within the political domain itself to achieve a more equal distribution of political power. Reforms should be implemented specifically within domain ***C*** of Figure 1.5, aiming for greater equity by empowering the low-income class to counterbalance the political sway of the wealthy. Instead of restricting the political power of the affluent, the contention is that reform should move toward augmenting the resilience of the low-income group despite having limited political resources. Schmitt asserts that by expanding political opportunities in this manner, the lower-income segment will attain a more potent political voice (**ii** in Table 6.2). In elections, all candidates should be granted equal opportunities for political expression, irrespective of their level of support or endorsement from the affluent classes. Additionally, it is crucial to ensure that all citizens can participate in the political process in diverse forms, going beyond their role as mere voters, including as donors, volunteers, and members of organizations. Individuals should have the freedom to express their political beliefs without facing suppression, and the political system should be structured in a way that emphasizes organizational influence rather than financial means, particularly regarding specific issues.

A democratic society can be comprehended as an intricate framework where diverse subsystems—such as civil society, economic society, political society, and the state—are intrinsically interconnected. Consequently, if one element becomes overly dominant or undemocratic, it obstructs the progress and democratization of other elements. For instance, an excessive presence of the state in a society obstructs the advancement of civil society, while the erosion of democratic principles within the economy, particularly in the business sector, undermines and contaminates both the state and political society. Acknowledging these challenges, Zingales strives to establish political democratization and transparency through economic democratization, with a special focus on nurturing corporate democratization. Conversely, Jacobs and Schmitt aim to achieve the democratization of the economic society and prevent the overactivation of the economic society by activating an underactive civil society. In essence, every aspect of a democratic society endeavors to restore harmony among its subdivisions by resolving conflicts through checks, division of power, and resource sharing.

Differing from the above-mentioned approaches, which seek to temporarily enhance power distribution for the low-income group, an alternative approach is to pursue a more enduring enhancement in power distribution at ***C*** in Figure 1.5 that benefits the low-income group through modifications to the political and electoral systems. If policies are crafted solely based on the existing power distribution scenario, without integrating institutionalization or system change, then as this power distribution changes over time, policies currently favoring the low-income group might be adjusted or annulled in the future. Hence, an argument exists that the central aspect of political reform should revolve around establishing a system capable of consistently representing the perspectives of the low-income class. Institutionalization is seen as a commitment device that solidifies compromises between political and social factions in an irreversible manner (Acemoglu and Robinson, 2006). Iversen and Soskice (2009), as well as Seon (2015), present this argument as a response to scenarios ② and ⑤ outlined in Table 6.1, aligning with the discourse on the variety of capitalism. They highlight that even within the same democratic framework, variations in inequality and redistribution persist due to disparities in political institutions such as the electoral system, party configuration, and governmental structure that constitute the democratic system. Their focus lies in understanding the impact of these political institutions on redistribution, with a particular emphasis on the electoral system, which mirrors the nature of the party system (two-party/majority party) and political alliances (unitary government/coalition government) through the majority system/proportional representation system. This is underlined as a defining aspect (**iv** in Table 6.2).

Regarding ⑤ in Table 6.1, to achieve a more equitable distribution of power within the political domain, it's imperative to institutionalize a pathway that allows the interests of diverse groups and classes to be equally and effectively integrated into the political process. The proponents believe that a combination of proportional representation and a multi-party system will likely lead to the emergence of a center-left coalition government. In essence, this creates a political landscape that is more amenable to institutionalizing and legislating matters of redistribution and welfare, in contrast to a majority-two-party combination that predominantly caters to the preferences of the median voter. This potential is emphasized (**x** in Table 6.2). Concerning ② in Table 6.1, it's highlighted that in a multi-party system, given that each party's development is primarily driven by economic cleavage, the feasibility of privatizing conflicts is minimal. Hence, their argument revolves around prioritizing the establishment of a framework for a consensus-driven political system that can encompass the perspectives of diverse classes through power-sharing arrangements, before delving into the formulation of intricate policies. This approach is advocated to effectively address the issue of redistribution.

Lastly, in relation to ③ outlined in Table 6.1, which involves creating a novel policy regime, Leighton and López (2013), Rodrik (2014), and Bresser-Pereira (2014) draw from Keynes–Hayek's discourse on policy formulation. They accentuate the significance of task specialization and collaboration among intellectuals, politicians, and knowledge brokers. As a result, they direct their focus toward the process of endogenous innovation, wherein collaborative intellectual efforts and the division of labor contribute to the emergence of innovative policy solutions (**vi** in Table 6.2).

Keynes concludes the *General Theory* by emphasizing the central role that ideas generated by philosophers and theorists play in the process of societal change.

> But apart from this contemporary mood, the ideas of economists and political philosophers, both when they are right and when they are wrong, are more powerful than is commonly understood. Indeed, the world is ruled by little else. Practical men, who believe themselves to be quite exempt from any intellectual influences, are usually the slaves of some defunct economist. Madmen in authority, who hear voices in the air, are distilling their frenzy from some academic scribbler of a few years back.
>
> (Keynes, 1936, p. 383)

In the excerpt quoted above, the term 'madman in authority' denotes not only the policy maker responsible for policy enforcement and rule alteration, but also includes politicians, bureaucrats, and other decision-makers within the political domain. Additionally, "academic scribblers," as coined by Keynes, are individuals who earn their livelihood by generating novel ideas, including philosophers, economists, and thinkers. As evident from the quoted passage, Keynes suggests that when these philosophers and economists introduce fresh concepts, there's a top-down effect wherein politicians and bureaucrats empathize with these ideas, leading to the creation of new regulations, policies, and institutions akin to the innovative endeavors of entrepreneurs. Similarly aligned with Keynes, Hayek concurs that the inception of novel policies or institutions follows a top-down trajectory. However, Hayek introduces a cadre of intellectuals termed "knowledge brokers." These actors take on an active role in curating and disseminating groundbreaking ideas among the very scholars and politicians who conceive them. These knowledge brokers, including journalists, critics, broadcasters, film directors, novelists, and columnists, have the mission of discerning the significance of emergent concepts and vetting them, not unlike creating new ideas. Their role extends to simplifying the core essence and significance of these concepts for public consumption. Leighton and López, Rodrik and Pereira lend their support to the dialogue presented by Keynes and Hayek concerning policy evolution, culminating in the rise of a renewed policy framework. A cohort of intellectuals, equipped with the capacity to evaluate existing policies critically and introduce innovative and original concepts, akin to scholars in essence, collaborates with skilled political leaders proficient in forging fresh class coalitions (echoing Keynes' notion of the 'madmen in authority'). Moreover, the media, often analogous to Hayek's knowledge brokers, assumes a pivotal role within this context. Furthermore, Pereira introduces an additional aspect by integrating international organizations into the discussion. He underscores the noteworthy role that conditional support from entities like the IMF or the World Bank assumes, especially during crises faced by developing nations. This assistance significantly contributes to shaping a novel policy framework.

Should this division of intellectual labor and collaborative endeavor result in the successful execution of policy innovation, the resultant fresh policy regime could effectively rationalize a more equitable redistribution of income and government intervention. Consequently, the distribution of political power within C in Figure 1.5, as previously explored, would lean toward increased parity. Furthermore, if these innovative policy measures adeptly balance heightened efficiency for the affluent upper class with augmented redistribution for the middle- and lower-income segments, akin to the welfare systems found in Nordic countries, the very notion of redistribution evolves beyond a mere transfer of income from one societal stratum to another. It transforms into a mechanism that ensures both efficacy and impartiality through the enhancement of productivity.

References

Acemoglu, D. and J. Robinson (2008), "Persistence of power, elites, and institutions," *American Economic Review*, Vol. 98, No. 1, pp. 267–269.

Acemoglu, D. and J. Robinson (2006), *Economic origins of dictatorship and democracy*, New York: Cambridge University Press.

Algan, Y., P. Cahuc, and M. Sangnier (2016, "Trust and the welfare state: The twin peaks curve," *Economic Journal*, Vol. 126, No. 593, pp. 861–883.

Bartel, L. (2008), *Unequal democracy: The political economy of a new gilded age*, Princeton, NJ: Princeton University Press.

Bresser-Pereira, L. C. (2014), "The hegemony constraints in the neoliberal years of capitalism," in Magara, E. (Ed), *Economic crises and policy regimes*, pp. 56–78, Cheltenham: Edward Elgar Publishing Limited.

Corak, M. (2013), "Income inequality, equality of opportunity, and intergenerational mobility," *Journal of Economic Perspectives*, Vol. 27, No. 3, pp. 79–102.

Ferreira, F. and V. Peragine (2015), "Equality of opportunity: Theory and evidence," *Policy Research Working Paper*, No. 7217, World Bank.
Gilens M. (2005), "Inequality and democratic responsiveness," *Public Opinion Quarterly*, Vol. 69, No. 5, pp. 778–796.
Hacker, J. and P. Pierson (2010), *Winner-take-all politics: How Washington made the rich richer and turned its back on the middle Class*, New York: Simon & Schuster Paperbacks.
Hall, P. A. and D. Soskice (2001), *Varieties of capitalism: The institutional foundations of comparative advantage*, Oxford: Oxford University Press.
Iversen, T. and D. Soskice (2009), "Distribution and redistribution: The shadow of the nineteenth century," *World Politics*, Vol. 61, No. 3, pp. 438–486.
Jacobs, E. (2017), "Everywhere and nowhere: Politics in capital in the twenty-first century," in Boushey, H., J. B. Delong, and M. Steinbaum (eds), *After Piketty: The Agenda for economics and inequality*, Cambridge, MA: Harvard University Press.
Keynes, J.M. (1936), *The general theory of employment, interest and money*, London: Macmillan and Co., Limited.
Leighton, W. A. and E. J. López (2013), *Madmen, intellectuals, and academic scribblers: The economic engine of political change*, Stanford, CA: Stanford University Press.
Lijphart, A. (2012), *Patterns of democracy: Government forms and performance in thirty-six countries*, New Haven: Yale University Press.
Przeworski, A. (2014), "Choices and echoes: Stability and change of policy regimes," in Magara, E. (Ed), *Economic crises and policy regimes*, pp 33–55, Cheltenham: Edward Elgar Publishing Limited.
Rodrik, D. (2014), "When ideas trump interests: Preferences, worldviews, and policy innovations," *Journal of Economic Perspectives*, Vol. 28, No. 1, pp. 189–208.
Rodrik, D. (1999), "Democracies pay higher wages," *Quarterly Journal of Economics*, Vol. 114, No. 3, pp. 707–738.
Rodrik, D. and S. Mukand (2016), "Ideas versus interests: A unified political economy framework," http://j.mp/2ovA6Zu
Rothstein, B. (2005), *Social traps and the problem of trust*, Cambridge: Cambridge University Press.
Schattschneider, E. E. (1960), *The semisovereign people: A realist view of democracy in America*, New York: Holt, Rinehart and Winston.
Schimitt, M. (2015), "Political opportunity: A new framework for democratic reform," *Brennan Center for Justice Working Paper.*
Seon, H. (2015), *The dynamics of consensus democracy*, Gwangju: Chon Nam National University Press.
Simpson, M. (1990), "Political rights and income inequality: A cross-national test," *American Sociological Review*, Vol. 55, No. 5, pp. 682–693.
Stiglitz, J. E. (2012), *The price of inequality: How today's divided society endangers our future*, New York: W.W. Norton & Company.
Zingales, L., (2017), "Towards a political theory of the firm," *NBER Working Paper Series*, No. 23593.

Index

Pages in **bold** refer to tables.

For Product Safety Concerns and Information please contact our EU
representative GPSR@taylorandfrancis.com
Taylor & Francis Verlag GmbH, Kaufingerstraße 24, 80331 München, Germany

www.ingramcontent.com/pod-product-compliance
Ingram Content Group UK Ltd.
Pitfield, Milton Keynes, MK11 3LW, UK
UKHW020000200926
475702UK00015B/2396

* 9 7 8 1 0 3 2 6 9 5 7 6 1 *